Cook in Boots

RAVINDER BHOGAL

Cook in Boots

Over 150 delectable recipes
Greed has never been so fashionable

Photography by Jason Lowe

HarperCollins*Publishers*

For my Grandfather – thank you – your blessings are always with us, and to my mother who gave me the best education she knew.

HarperCollinsPublishers
77–85 Fulham Palace Road,
Hammersmith, London W6 8JB

www.harpercollins.co.uk

First published by HarperCollinsPublishers 2009

10 9 8 7 6 5 4 3 2 1

© Ravinder Bhogal 2009

Ravinder Bhogal asserts the moral right to be
identified as the author of this work

Photography © Jason Lowe
Food styling: Ravinder Bhogal
Prop styling: Cynthia Inions
Home economist: Lori de Mori
Hair and make-up: Irena Rogers and Sonia Deveney
Photographs pp 71, 83, 167, 181, 299 © R. Ahmad

A catalogue record of this book is
available from the British Library

ISBN 978-0-00-729117-5

Printed and bound in Great Britain by
Butler Tanner & Dennis Ltd, Frome, Somerset

Contents

Chapter One

BREAD, PASTA, POTATOES: Fall off the carb-free wagon 14

Chapter Two

WORKING IT 9–5: Work to live, live to eat 49

Chapter Three

COMFORT FOOD: When you've got no one to give you a hug, you need a hug on a plate 69

Chapter Four

PMT: For the times when only chocolate will do 93

Chapter Five

TV, REMOTE CONTROL AND A MEAL FOR ONE: We all need a little me-time 111

Chapter Six

SOCIAL GRAZING: Lots of Martinis and food to pick at   129

Chapter Seven

HANGOVER FOOD: For the morning after the night before   157

Chapter Eight

HARD-UP FOOD: For when you've spent all your lolly on your Louboutins 179

Chapter Nine

SKINNY FOOD: For when you feel the pinch of the Chloe jeans 195

Chapter Ten

FOOD REHAB: No need to go cold turkey

Power Eating

Superfoods to the Rescue

Chapter Eleven

FORK ME, SPOON ME: The food of love and rude food

This'll Get You Going...

The Main Event

Room 4 Dessert

Chapter Twelve

Cook's notes

Season with sea salt and freshly ground black pepper unless otherwise stated.

Use large eggs, preferably free range and organic. Avoid recipes with raw egg if you are pregnant.

Use the zest of unwaxed oranges and lemons.

Use free range and preferably organic meat and poultry.

Try to buy responsibly sourced fish. See http://rfs.seafish.org for more details or get your fishmonger to try and suggest alternatives for fish with depleted stocks.

DEEP-FRYING

1 Choose oils with a high smoke point, such as groundnut, sunflower and peanut oil.

2 Oil and water don't mix, so make sure any foods you fry are as dry as they can be, otherwise the oil will spit.

3 Use enough oil for your food to float in; it shouldn't touch the bottom of the pan.

4 The oil is hot enough to cook in when a dice-sized cube of bread plunged into it browns in 1 minute.

5 Don't overcrowd the pan or the temperature of the oil will drop.

Introduction

What do I like to eat? Everything. Any time.

I am not a chef – just a rather enthusiastic domestic cook and greedy girl about town. My recipes do not come from years of sweating over a hot hob, but rather from my own need to indulge my voracious appetite. I find myself constantly deep in gastronomic meditation – whether I am fantasising about a deep dish of fragrant curry dotted with coriander, or a jewel-coloured cocktail jelly, my culinary imagination keeps me salivating and therefore cooking.

I refuse to bend to foodie trends or flavours of the month. What I cook is dictated by mood. If I am sick, I want nothing more than a bowl of chicken noodle soup, or if I find myself dumped by a lover, chocolate pudding quickly becomes his substitute.

Women – strange, empathetic, subjective and intuitive creatures that we are – need a book that accords with our multi-mood lifestyle. When the men, or women, in our life don't understand us, we need a book that does. Something to answer all our needs and address all of our appetites!

This book does exactly that; it's structured not only around the demands of the stomach, but the head and the heart too. Let's face it – sometimes picking up a spoon full of chocolate ice cream has more to do with feeding the soul than the stomach.

Cook in Boots is split into 12 chapters, targeting the areas in our lives that we most need help with. It easily switches from practical manual – cooking on a shoestring budget or feeding the hangover monster – to being your indulgent substitute partner in crime with chocolate-centric cuisine and rude food. Whatever craving you are looking to satisfy, *Cook in Boots* provides the perfect recipe. There are over 150 of them to choose from, so by all means whip them up, or just look at the pictures and drool.

CHAPTER ONE

Bread, pasta, potatoes

Fall off the carb-free wagon

The Zone. The GI. The Cabbage Soup. If you're a yo-yo dieter at all, you've probably had a bash at one or all of the above – and most likely the Atkins. No pasta, no fries, no cakes, not even a teeny mouthful of your boyfriend's bacon sandwich. Jealous? Well, of course – especially of restaurant diners gorging on forbidden bread baskets.

I remember well the smugness of feeling it work. The skinny jeans you bought on a thin day – and wore just once – start to fit without the battle of shifting around the overhang. Like magic, your muffin top moulds itself into a cinched little waist, and your thighs are so divine in that Marni mini dress, you daringly ask your dry cleaner to take it up an extra half inch.

But how can we talk about the dark days of Atkins without a mention of lo-carb lows? Extreme hunger cramps, palpitations, irrational mood swings and a broken-hearted pining for a simple ploughman's sandwich.

I happily fell off the wagon a long time ago, and I may be half a stone heavier for it, but at least I can enjoy a bagel without the dough guilt. Please, I urge you, grab a fork and have a little linguine. Re-enter the world of real food. It's a pretty delicious place!

GRILLED COURGETTE & BUFFALO MOZZARELLA PANZANELLA

Falling off the Atkins needn't mean that you have to go on a crazed carbs binge, but it does mean you don't have to dodge the croutons.

This tasty salad celebrates bread by making it the main feature of the dish rather than just a paltry garnish. It's great for using up any stale loaves you may have knocking around, and makes perfect picnic fodder. I do admit that I sometimes make it just as an excuse to eat half a loaf of bread, veiled in the righteousness of eating salad.

Toss the bread, onion, tomatoes, capers, basil and mozzarella into a large salad bowl.

In a small bowl, whisk together the olive oil, chilli flakes and sugar and then anoint the sliced courgettes with it. Heat a griddle or frying pan until very hot, then place the courgettes on it in a single layer. Once they are softened and charred on both sides, toss them into the salad bowl.

Make the dressing by whisking together all the ingredients and then pour over the salad an hour before you are ready to serve it up. The bread should have picked up some of the juices, but it shouldn't be soggy.

SERVES 4

1 small, day-old ciabatta loaf, cut into 2cm/¾in cubes
1 red onion, finely sliced into crescents
3 very ripe tomatoes, each quartered and quartered again to give 8 pieces
2 tsp capers
1 handful of fresh basil leaves, torn
125g/4oz buffalo mozzarella cheese, torn into bite-sized hunks
1 tbsp olive oil
½ tsp chilli flakes
1 tsp caster sugar
2 courgettes, trimmed and thinly sliced lengthways

For the dressing
4 tbsp extra virgin olive oil
2 tbsp red wine vinegar
1 tsp caster sugar
sea salt and freshly ground black pepper

KITCHEN-ADE
If you don't love courgettes, try griddled radicchio or fennel instead.

CRAB, WATERCRESS & POTATO SALAD

A bowlful of this is a reassuring reminder that summer is almost here.

SERVES 4

500g/1lb 2oz new potatoes, such as Jersey Royals, scrubbed
2 handfuls of watercress
300ml/10fl oz crème fraîche
juice of 1 large lime
2 heaped tbsp capers, drained or rinsed
2 heaped tbsp fresh flat-leaf parsley
½ tsp cayenne pepper
sea salt and freshly ground black pepper
200g/7oz fresh cooked crab meat

This salad is particularly delightful eating in March when Jersey Royals are newly in season. Of course, you can use any other type of new potato, but there is something extra special about the pairing of a panful of new Jerseys, as perfect as polished pebbles, and fresh sweet crab meat.

Cook the potatoes in plenty of simmering salted water until they are tender. Drain and chop them into bite-sized pieces. Place them in a bowl along with the watercress, which should wilt slightly in their residual heat.

In a separate bowl, mix the crème fraîche with the lime juice, capers, parsley, cayenne pepper and seasoning to make the dressing.

Once the potatoes are cool, toss in the juicy lumps of crab meat and then pour the creamy dressing over them. Mix well and either eat immediately with a glass of very cold, well-deserved sparkling white wine, or refrigerate until you are ready.

KITCHEN-ADE

Jersey Royals are delicate little potatoes and are quite easy to overcook. This amount should take between 8 and 10 minutes to cook, but be watchful. Overcooking them is not an entire disaster, but it is a shame.

Crab meat is readily available in supermarkets and your local fishmongers, but I like to hunt it down at those traditional fish shacks outside pubs. You know, the ones that sell everything from jellied eels to cockles in malt vinegar. They're fading fast now, but they're such a great British tradition that it's important to support them. They tend to open Thursday through to Sunday, so the produce is always fresh, and in my experience they always cut you a fair deal.

FATTOUSH

One mouthful of the crunchy fried flat bread and the tongue-smarting sumac had me hooked.

As a student, my nights out often ended with a pit stop at Edgware Road's all-night Lebanese restaurants to sate my midnight munchies. This is where I first discovered fattoush. Nowadays, I tend to make a bowlful of this refreshing salad at least once a week, if anything because I hate to waste food and this accounts nicely for any pitta breads on their way out.

In a bowl, combine the lettuce, cucumber, tomatoes, parsley, mint, green pepper, radishes and garlic. Snip the bread into rough bite-sized pieces – this is best done with a pair of scissors for speed.

Heat the olive oil in a frying pan and fry the bread in batches until golden brown and crackly. Drain on kitchen paper to remove any excess oil. Dress the salad with the extra virgin olive oil and lemon juice and then sprinkle with the tangy sumac seeds and season. Finally, toss in the fried bread and give it a good mix. Serve piled high on a plate with some extra curls of lettuce.

KITCHEN-ADE

Sumac is a ground condiment made from dried red berries and has an acerbic sherbet tang. It is readily available in Middle Eastern grocery shops, but if you have trouble getting hold of it you can order online at www.thespiceshop.co.uk or www.seasonedpioneers.co.uk.

To make more of a meal of your fattoush, crumble some salty feta cheese over before serving.

SERVES 4

1 romaine lettuce, torn, plus extra leaves to serve
1 Lebanese cucumber, quartered lengthways then chopped
3 good tomatoes, each quartered and quartered again to give 8 pieces
1 bunch of fresh flat-leaf parsley, chopped
1 bunch of fresh mint, chopped
½ green pepper, deseeded and finely sliced
15 radishes, thinly sliced
1 garlic clove, finely chopped
2 Middle Eastern flatbreads or pitta breads
2 tbsp olive oil
8 tbsp extra virgin olive oil
juice of 1 lemon
1 tsp sumac (see Kitchen-ade)
sea salt and freshly ground black pepper

SWEET POTATO SALAD WITH LIME, CORIANDER & SWEET CHILLI DRESSING

I love to serve it on a large blue plate so that the flame-fleshed sweet potatoes really stand out.

SERVES 4–6

3 long orange-fleshed sweet
    potatoes, peeled and
    chopped into 1cm/½in
    discs
6 tbsp sweet chilli sauce
1 medium red onion,
    chopped ultra fine
    (mind your fingers!)
3 heaped tbsp chopped fresh
    coriander
juice of 1 ripe lime

This vibrant salad is as appealing to the eye as it is to the stomach, and it's as good on its own as it is with grilled fish or meat. It takes no time or real effort to knock it up and the taste improves the longer you leave it. I always make more than I need and eat it straight out of the refrigerator the next day.

Steam the discs of potato until they are tender but still firm – 10–15 minutes. Lay them out on a serving platter and pour the sweet chilli sauce evenly over them. Now, scatter on the onion and coriander and finish off the dish with a healthy squirt of lime juice. You can eat this immediately, but it is better left for a couple of hours, when the sweet potatoes have really soaked up all the flavours of the dressing – patience is a virtue after all!

KITCHEN-ADE

Don't boil the sweet potatoes – they tend to fall apart. Steaming is the best method, although, at a pinch, you can microwave them with their skins on – cook on Full Power for 5 minutes.

FRIED CASSAVA WITH SPICY SALT, CORIANDER & LIME JUICE

This easy peasy dish is great to knock up when you have friends over for supper.

SERVES 6

2 large cassava tubers, peeled and chopped into thick wedges
groundnut oil for deep-frying (see Kitchen-ade below)
1 red onion, diced as finely as possible
1 handful of chopped fresh coriander
1 tsp caster sugar
sea salt
½ tsp chilli flakes
juice of 1 large lime

Cassava, yuca or mogo, as it is also called, is a starchy root that is a major source of carbs. It's hardly eaten at all by the British, but is massively popular in Africa where I grew up. Once you get beyond the strange tuber shape and waxy brown skin, it can be cooked in more or less the same way as potatoes. In fact, a tray of roast cassava is every bit as delicious as more traditional roasties.

Boil the cassava in plenty of salted water until tender – this should take about 25 minutes. Drain and then chop the wedges into 2cm/¾in cubes.

Heat the groundnut oil in a deep-fat fryer and deep-fry the cassava in small batches, to ensure the oil stays hot, until golden and crispy. Drain on kitchen paper to remove any excess oil.

Place the fried cassava in a bowl with the onion and coriander. Pound together the sugar, 1 teaspoon salt and the chilli flakes in a pestle and mortar to make a chilli salt. Sprinkle the salt over the cassava and then squeeze plenty of lime juice over. Toss well and serve warm or cold.

KITCHEN-ADE

For a healthier version of this, heat the oven to 200°C/400°F/gas 6, brush the cassava wedges with olive oil and bake for 30 minutes or until golden brown all over. Then mix with all the other ingredients as above.

Cassava is widely available in Indian and African supermarkets. When selecting your cassava, make sure you pick ones that feel firm and are unblemished. It is also available in the freezer section, conveniently peeled and parboiled.

SMOKED SALMON, BEETROOT & HORSERADISH BAGEL

The fiery kiss of the horseradish, the saltiness of the smoked salmon and the piquant tang of the beetroot make this bagel a real breadwinner!

Smoked salmon and cream cheese is a classic combination, but sometimes I just want something that has a little more kick, which is why I love this.

This is not so much cooking as an assembly job. Split the bagels and toast them. Mix the soured cream and horseradish together and season with pepper, then spread generously over the four surfaces of the bagels. Top with the watercress, then drape the salmon over. Add the beetroot, then another milling of pepper and a squirt of lemon juice. Enjoy!

SERVES 2

2 bagels
2 heaped tbsp soured cream
1 heaped tbsp horseradish sauce
freshly ground black pepper
1 handful of watercress
6 slices of smoked salmon
2 small cooked preserved
    beetroots (not in vinegar),
    sliced
juice of ½ lemon

HALLOUMI & SWEET BALSAMIC TOMATO OPEN SANDWICH

I adore halloumi in all its salty, squeaky, pallid glory.

SERVES 2

4–6 vine-ripened tomatoes,
    halved lengthways
olive oil and thick syrupy
    balsamic vinegar, to
    drizzle
4 garlic cloves, 3 finely
    chopped and 1 left whole
leaves stripped from 3 sprigs
    of thyme, chopped
1 tsp dried oregano
2 tsp caster sugar
sea salt and freshly ground
    black pepper
200g/7oz halloumi cheese,
    sliced
4 thick slices of ciabatta
    bread
2 tbsp chopped fresh flat-leaf
    parsley

The thing that makes this cheese different from many others is the way it holds its shape, making it perfect for barbecuing, frying, or grilling as I have for this sandwich. Its natural saltiness works particularly well with the bursting sweet and sourness of the ripe grilled tomatoes here.

Preheat the grill to medium. Drizzle the tomatoes with a little olive oil and 1 tablespoon of balsamic vinegar, then sprinkle with the chopped garlic, thyme, oregano, sugar and seasoning. Grill for 10 minutes until they are bursting and caramelised but still holding their shape.

Heat a griddle pan until very hot, then lay the sliced halloumi on it. Cook on both sides until crisp and branded with zebra stripes.

Rub both sides of the ciabatta slices with the whole garlic clove, sprinkle with olive oil and then cook on the griddle until they are crisp and golden.

Layer the halloumi on the bread and top with the tomatoes. Dress with a little parsley and another drizzle of olive oil and balsamic vinegar and serve.

KITCHEN-ADE

The quality of halloumi can vary. Look out for 'village halloumi' made from either goat's or sheep's milk. It has a superior flavour to cow's milk halloumi, which is mass-produced in factories.

PAPRIKA PRAWNS ON SOURDOUGH TOAST WITH ROCKET

I love this combination of sweet juicy prawns with the intense smokiness of paprika, its deep husky edge taken off by the soured cream.

Piling the prawns up on sourdough toast like this means that the bread soaks up all the spicy juices, so you don't waste a scrap of flavour.

Warm the olive oil in a pan with the garlic. When the garlic colours, add the paprika. A minute later, add the prawns and salt and pepper to taste. As the prawns begin to take colour, pour in the brandy and ignite. Finish by pouring in the cream, then warm through and scatter with parsley. Serve heaped on sourdough toast with a handful of rocket.

SERVES 2

1 tbsp olive oil
2 garlic cloves, chopped
1 tsp smoked hot paprika
16 raw tiger prawns, peeled and deveined
sea salt and freshly ground black pepper
1 tbsp brandy
30ml/generous 1fl oz soured cream
1 tbsp chopped fresh flat-leaf parsley
2 slices of sourdough toast
1 handful of rocket, to serve

GRIDDLED SARDINE BRUSCHETTA WITH TOMATO & BASIL

I love sardines – they are cheap, abundant, good for you and cook in absolutely no time at all.

Eating them in this way with perfumed basil, zesty lemons and ripe tomatoes reminds me of long lunches by the sea and always puts me in a 'holiday' mood – no air miles required. Get your fishmonger to remove the sardine heads and gut them for you, but if you fancy having a go yourself, just chop off their heads, make a split in their bellies, scrape out their innards and rinse.

An hour or so before you're ready to cook, make the dressing by simply steeping the onion in the olive oil, balsamic vinegar, lemon juice, oregano and salt. The acidity will make the onions soft and translucent and take away any acrid flavour, leaving them mellow and sweet.

Heat a griddle or frying pan until very hot. Brush the sardines with a little olive oil and season with salt and pepper. Rub the bread with the garlic and sprinkle with some olive oil. Put both the fish and the bread on the griddle and cook for 2 minutes on each side or until the bread is golden and the sardines opaque-fleshed and charred.

Place the sardines on the bruschetta and top with the sliced tomatoes, onion dressing and, finally, some torn basil.

SERVES 2

4 small sardines, gutted
   and heads removed
olive oil
sea salt and freshly ground
   black pepper
2 slices from a large
   ciabatta loaf
1 garlic clove
2 vine-ripened tomatoes,
   sliced
a few fresh basil leaves, torn

For the dressing
½ red onion, sliced into
   fine rings
2 tbsp olive oil
1 tbsp balsamic vinegar
1 tbsp lemon juice
1 tsp dried oregano
a little sea salt

KITCHEN-ADE
For a seriously quick and convenient supper, swap the fresh sardines for tinned ones.

GOAN SAUSAGE BURGERS WITH CHILLI PINEAPPLE SALSA & MASALA CHIPS

This is a brilliant way to resurrect an old British favourite.

Whether pork served with pineapple is food hell or nostalgia on a plate for you, I urge you to try this lip-smackingly good burger with coriander, chilli and spices. Serve it up with a cheerful pineapple salsa and some more-ishly sticky masala chips, which have both the bolshy heat of chillies and the sweetness of jaggery. If you can't get hold of jaggery, try using soft brown sugar instead.

SERVES 6

For the Goan sausage burgers

3 fat garlic cloves, roughly chopped
1 thumb of fresh root ginger, peeled and
    roughly chopped (see Kitchen-ade)
500g/1lb 2oz lean pork mince
1 small red onion, finely chopped
1 red chilli (deseeded if you don't want
    it too spicy), finely sliced
1 tsp each of cumin and coriander
    seeds, both toasted in a dry pan
    and crushed
1 tsp mild Madras curry powder
zest and juice of 1 lemon
6 tbsp chopped fresh coriander
1 egg, beaten
sea salt and freshly ground
    black pepper
a little vegetable oil for
    shallow-frying

For the pineapple salsa

1 small pineapple
3 tbsp chopped fresh mint
1 red chilli (deseeded if you don't want
    it too spicy), finely chopped
3 tbsp chopped fresh coriander
juice of ½ lime
1 tsp mango powder (amchur, see
    Kitchen-ade, page 32)

For the masala chips

6 Desiree potatoes, peeled and cut into
    thick wedges
100g/3½oz jaggery or palm sugar
3 tbsp white wine vinegar
groundnut oil for deep-frying
    (see Cook's Notes, page 12)
2 tbsp vegetable oil
2 garlic cloves, crushed
2.5cm/1in knob of fresh root ginger,
    peeled and finely grated
½ tsp ground cinnamon
½ tsp chilli flakes

First, make the burgers. Put the garlic and ginger into a food processor and blitz to a fine paste. Mix the paste with the pork, onion, chilli, toasted crushed seeds, curry powder, lemon zest and juice and coriander, combining well, then add the beaten egg to bind. Let the mixture rest for about 30 minutes to allow the mince to absorb all the bold flavours. Only season with salt just before cooking or the onions will let out their water and the mixture will turn soggy.

Meanwhile, make your salsa. Peel and finely chop the pineapple. Combine with the mint, chilli and coriander – the colours here are just so vibrant and the flavour will be equally lively. Squeeze the lime over, season, mix well and then sprinkle with the mango powder.

Run the potato wedges under cold water to get rid of some of the starch – this will stop them sticking together. Wrap them in a tea towel to dry. Soak the jaggery or palm sugar in the vinegar and mix until it is more or less dissolved. There is no need to parboil the potatoes here – you want them to be firm for when you cook them again in the jaggery and vinegar. Heat the groundnut oil in a deep-fat fryer or a wok and fry the wedges in batches until they are golden and cooked through. Drain on kitchen paper.

Heat a little vegetable oil in a frying pan and then shape your sausage burgers. Take handfuls of the mixture, shape into a ball and then flatten out like a burger. Fry for 4–5 minutes on each side over a medium heat to cook them through, but still keep them succulent. Keep them warm while you finish making the masala chips.

In a separate pan or wok, heat the vegetable oil and fry the garlic and ginger with the cinnamon until golden and fragrant. Pour in the jaggery and vinegar and heat over a medium flame until it's golden and bubbling and most of the vinegar has evaporated. Sprinkle in the chilli flakes, mix once, and then throw in the chips and coat in the sticky spicy sauce. Serve at once with the burgers and pineapple salsa.

KITCHEN-ADE

I always peel the ginger with the side of a spoon – scraping off the skin rather than using a peeler, which wastes too much.

Amchur powder is available in all Indian food stores and gives a wonderful uplifting tang that is more subtle than lemon juice.

SWEET POTATO CAKES WITH TAMARIND CHICKPEA RELISH

As a dish, it falls into the category of 'chaat' – a type of Indian tapas, often eaten at tea time, that translates literally as 'to lick'. Judging by my strong urge to lap up my plate on finishing – it really is no surprise.

In India these potato cakes are traditionally made with standard potatoes, but I adore the flavour of saccharine, flame-fleshed sweet potatoes with the tang of the tamarind in the chickpea relish.

SERVES 6

For the sweet potato cakes
4 orange-fleshed sweet potatoes, peeled
   and chopped
4 garlic cloves, crushed
1 thumb of fresh root ginger, peeled
   and grated
1 red onion, finely chopped
2 green chillies (deseeded if you don't
   want it too spicy), finely chopped
1 tsp coarsely ground toasted cumin seeds
1 tsp coarsely ground toasted coriander
   seeds
sea salt and coarsely ground black pepper
6 tbsp chopped fresh coriander
50g/2oz breadcrumbs
1 heaped tbsp gram flour
groundnut oil for deep-frying
   (see Cook's Notes, page 12)
juice of ½ lime
Greek yoghurt, to serve

For the tamarind chickpea relish
1 tbsp vegetable oil
1 red onion, sliced
sea salt, to taste
½ tsp cumin seeds
seeds from 4 green cardamom pods,
   bashed
½ tsp coarsely ground black pepper
1 tbsp tomato purée
3 tbsp tamarind concentrate
50ml/2fl oz water
1 × 400g tin of chickpeas, drained
   and rinsed
1 handful of chopped fresh coriander
1 stick of cinnamon, crushed

Steam the sweet potatoes until they are tender. Put the garlic, ginger, onion, chillies and spices into a bowl and then mash in the sweet potatoes. Scatter in the coriander and then, using your hands, add the breadcrumbs and gram flour and knead well to bind. Let the mixture rest in the fridge for 30 minutes to firm up.

To make the relish, heat the vegetable oil in a pan and gently fry the onion, with a little salt to stop it browning, until just half cooked. Add the spices and pepper and fry again until they are aromatic – this should take no more than 2 minutes. Stir in the tomato purée, tamarind and water, then tumble in the chickpeas and toss well to coat in the glossy sauce. Simmer for 5 minutes until the sauce has thickened and reduced. Finish by speckling with the chopped coriander.

Heat the groundnut oil in a deep-fat fryer. Season the sweet potato mixture with salt and pour in the lime juice. Mix well and then fashion tablespoons of it into flat patties. This amount of mixture should make about 20, but you can never be precise.

Turn the heat under the oil down to medium and fry the patties until they are a nutty brown and crisp on the outside. Drain on kitchen paper to soak up any excess oil and then serve topped with the tart chickpea relish and a dollop of creamy Greek yoghurt.

TEMPURA FISH & CHIPS WITH PICKLED GINGER & WASABI MAYONNAISE

Here's my Japanese-inspired take on the English classic – no mushy peas required!

Thank goodness for Sir Walter Raleigh, who brought England the humble potato in the 16th century. I bet he never imagined just how passionate the English would get about a perfect stick of potato pleasure teamed with a fat, deep-fried fillet of fish.

SERVES 6

1kg/2¼lb white firm-fleshed fish
    (you can use pollack, cod, haddock,
    plaice or turbot – whatever you like),
    cut into 6 fat fillets

The perfect chip
6 large Desiree potatoes
1 tsp sea salt
1 litre/1¾ pints groundnut oil for
    deep-frying (see Cook's Notes, page 12)
sea salt flakes

For the tempura batter
50g/2oz plain flour
50g/2oz cornflour
1 tbsp baking powder
½ tsp sea salt
1 egg, beaten
200ml/7fl oz ice-cold sparkling
    water
1 ice cube

**For the pickled ginger and wasabi
mayonnaise**
6 heaped tbsp very good-quality mayonnaise
1 tbsp wasabi paste
1 tbsp rice wine vinegar
1 tsp caster sugar
3 tbsp finely chopped sliced pickled ginger

Timing is everything with this dish – this is not the kind of batter you can make in advance, it has to be made just before you're ready to cook with it, so I always do the chips and mayo first. Peel the potatoes and chop them into 1.5cm/²⁄₃in fingers – don't get out your geometry set, they don't have to be exact at all! Rinse them under cold water to get rid of some of the starch – this will stop them sticking together as they fry.

Bring plenty of water to the boil in a large pan, add the salt and then the potatoes. Boil them until the edges start to break down slightly – this is what is going to give your chips real crunch. It normally takes about 10 minutes to get to this point. Preheat the oven to low, 150°C/300°F/gas 2.

While your potatoes are on the boil, make the wasabi mayonnaise. This is not so much cooking as just mixing together all the ingredients. I love how with the addition of the hot wasabi the mayonnaise turns the palest shade of jade. It's really going to give your fish a kick!

Once the potatoes are ready, drain them and then get ready to fry. Heat the groundnut oil in a deep-fat fryer until it's almost smoking – test by putting a cube of bread into it. If the bread immediately rises to the surface and starts turning golden, it's ready.

Fry the chips in batches – don't overcrowd the pan or the temperature of the oil will fall and you won't get the crunch you're looking for. Once they are all fried, sprinkle with flakes of sea salt and keep them warm in the oven. Keep the oil heated while you prepare the fish.

Don't be frightened off by urban myths on tricky tempura batter – just remember the golden rules: keep the water ice cold and don't over-mix it – this does not need to be a smooth batter. I find mixing with a chopstick works the best. Begin by sifting both the flours and the baking powder into a mixing bowl. Add the salt. Mix the beaten egg and water together and then pour onto the flour and mix a few times – remember, don't overwork it! Pop in your ice cube.

Now the exciting part – the frying. I love the sound of the icy cold batter hitting the hot oil, it's like enthusiastic applause – you know your fish is going to be pretty damn good if there is already clapping for it! Dip the fish fillets into the batter, making sure they are well coated, and then pop into the oil and fry until golden, about 6 minutes. The batter should go crisp and lacy. Drain well and rest on kitchen paper.

Team with the chips and wasabi mayo and eat immediately, to make the most of the crispy batter – why would you want to wait anyway?

PIZZA

*'When the moon hits your eye, like a big pizza pie, that's amore.'
In fact, I have never met anybody who doesn't love pizza.*

MAKES 4 MEDIUM PIZZAS

For the dough

400g/14oz '00' Italian flour
    or strong white bread
    flour, plus extra to dust
100g/3½oz fine semolina
1 tsp sea salt
300ml/10fl oz warm water
2 tbsp olive oil, plus extra
    to grease
1 × 7g sachet of fast-action
    yeast
1 tsp honey

These ones are perfection – the crust is oven-charred and crisp, but still slightly chewy on the inside, and they have just the right ratio of topping, sauce and bubbling stringy cheese. The only other thing your heart could possibly desire is a cold beer to wash them down with. Could this be love?

Sift the flour and semolina into a large bowl and crumble in the salt. (You can stick to using just 500g/1lb 2oz '00' flour here, but the semolina really oomphs up crispiness in your base.) In a jug, mix together the water, olive oil, yeast and honey and then set aside for 15 minutes.

Make a well in the centre of the flour and pour in your liquid. Using the end of a spoon, slowly push the flour into the liquid, working it all in. Then dust your hands with flour, tip the dough out onto a work surface and knead until the dough is smooth and elastic. It should take about 8 minutes to reach this point, so bear with it.

Place the dough in a floured bowl, sprinkle with some more flour, then cover it with a damp cloth and leave in a warm place to rise for 1 hour. I tend to warm up my microwave and store the dough inside

Remove the dough from the bowl and knead again to knock all the air out of it. Divide it into four pieces and roll each piece into a rough circle about 20cm/8in across.

TO COOK ALL PIZZAS

To cook, preheat the grill to very hot. Place each pizza base on oiled squares of foil and grill for 5 minutes. Flip over and layer with your chosen topping (see pages 40–42) and bake in a preheated oven at 230°C/450°F/gas 8. Grilling it before baking like this ensures an extra crispy base – and gives the effect of having cooked it in a wood-burning oven.

TOPPINGS

My favourite tomato sauce

1 slug of olive oil for frying
½ onion, finely chopped
2 garlic cloves, finely
    chopped
1 × 400g tin of tomatoes
1 tsp caster sugar
2 tbsp sun-dried tomato
    paste
2 tbsp torn fresh basil leaves
sea salt and freshly ground
    black pepper

Heat the olive oil and then fry the onion until it is soft but still pale. Stir in the garlic and fry for 2 minutes, then pour in the tomatoes and add the sugar. Simmer on a low heat for 20 minutes until the sauce has thickened and reduced. Stir in the tomato paste, fresh basil and season to taste.

Pesto

30g/generous 1oz pine nuts,
    lightly toasted in a dry pan
1 garlic clove
1 tsp sea salt
leaves stripped from 1 large
    bunch of basil
50g/2oz freshly grated
    Parmesan cheese
200ml/7fl oz extra virgin
    olive oil
2 tbsp lemon juice

Heat a pan and lightly toast the pine nuts, making sure you take them off the heat once they are pale golden.

In a pestle and mortar, crush the garlic together with the salt and then add the pine nuts. Bash until you have a coarse crumble, then add the basil and pound again. Stir in the cheese, and pour in the extra virgin olive oil in a steady stream until it is a consistency you are happy with – it should be neither too runny nor too stiff. Finish with a little lemon juice to really lift the flavour.

To store the pesto, pour it into a jar and pour a layer of olive oil over the surface. Cover and refrigerate – it will keep for up to a week.

KITCHEN-ADE

If you are feeling a little less energetic, in place of using a pestle and mortar, you can throw all the ingredients into a food processor and whiz, but there is an added deliciousness to the better texture of a hand-pounded pesto.

Chorizo and mushroom pizza

Preheat your grill to medium. Smear your pizza base with the tomato sauce, leaving a border for the crust. Top with chorizo, mozzarella, onion and mushrooms and bake in the oven for 12–15 minutes.

3 tbsp tomato sauce
100g/3½oz uncooked chorizo, sliced
100g/3½oz mozzarella cheese, grated
½ red onion, sliced thinly into crescents
8 large chestnut mushrooms, thinly sliced

Pizza with potatoes and thyme

Boil the potatoes in plenty of salted water for 5–7 minutes and then drain. Drizzle with 1 tablespoon of the olive oil and then throw in the garlic and thyme and toss well.

Arrange potato slices over the ungrilled side of your pizza base, leaving a border for the crust. Top with the goat's cheese, drizzle with the remaining olive oil and bake for 15 minutes until the potatoes and the cheese are oven-singed.

15 small waxy potatoes, thinly sliced
sea salt
2 tbsp olive oil
2 garlic cloves, chopped
leaves stripped from 5 sprigs of thyme
125g/4oz soft goat's cheese, sliced

Pesto pizza with mozzarella and marinated tomatoes

4 ripe tomatoes, sliced

1 tsp caster sugar

sea salt and freshly ground
   black pepper

2 garlic cloves, finely sliced

10 fresh basil leaves, torn

extra virgin olive oil and aged
   balsamic vinegar, to drizzle

2 tbsp fresh pesto
   (see page 40)

150g ball of buffalo
   mozzarella cheese

Lay the tomatoes in a single layer in a flat dish and sprinkle with the sugar and salt and pepper to taste. Scatter the garlic and basil leaves on top and then drizzle with the extra virgin olive oil and balsamic vinegar. Leave to marinate for at least 20 minutes.

Once you have grilled one side of the pizza, flip it over and smear the pesto over the ungrilled side, leaving a border for the crust. Bake in the oven for 15 minutes. Remove from the oven, top with the marinated tomatoes and the mozzarella, drizzle with extra virgin olive oil and a little balsamic vinegar and serve.

Harissa and halloumi pizza

2 tbsp harissa paste

200g/7oz halloumi cheese,
   sliced crossways

50g/2oz kalamata olives

extra virgin olive oil, to drizzle

2 tbsp chopped fresh flat-leaf
   parsley

Smooth the harissa paste all over the ungrilled side of the base, leaving a border for the crust. Top with the halloumi and olives and then drizzle with the extra virgin olive oil. Bake in the oven for 15 minutes and then scatter with the parsley before serving.

KITCHEN-ADE

Harissa paste is a North African sauce made from dried red chillies, garlic, tomatoes and spices. It is served as a condiment or used in stews. It is widely available in tins, jars and tubes in a variety of hotness – the best and most tongue-numbingly hot variety I have come across comes in tins and jars from Tunisia. Try Le Phare du Cap Bon (www.chilliworld.com) but be warned, handle with caution.

MORE-ISH PARMESAN-GARLIC BREAD

Garlic bread is not just dough — it's the toast with the most.

Unsurprisingly, the main difference between a good and average garlic bread is the quality of loaf used — I recommend using either a thick-crusted Italian ciabatta or a long thin French baguette. There are few better ways to my mind of getting your carb fix than chomping through slice after slice of oozing garlic butter and Parmesan cheese on chewy, open-textured bread. This one also packs in enough blood-thinning garlic to balance the generous amount of butter used, so your arteries shouldn't feel too bad!

Preheat the oven to 200°C/400°F/gas 6. Cream together the butter, garlic, oregano, seasoning and half the Parmesan cheese.

Using a sharp knife, make diagonal incisions in the loaf about 3cm/1¼in apart, as if you were slicing the loaf, but don't cut it right through. Take a sheet of kitchen foil large enough to parcel the loaf and place the loaf in the middle. Using a knife, smear the garlic butter between the slices and then sprinkle the remaining cheese between the slices. Close up the parcel and bake for 10 minutes, then open it up and bake for a further 5 minutes to get a brisk-to-the-bite crust.

MAKES 1 LOAF

150g/5oz unsalted butter, at room temperature
1 tbsp crushed garlic
1 tsp dried oregano
sea salt and freshly ground black pepper
25g/1oz Parmesan cheese, grated
1 large ciabatta loaf or French baguette

GOAT'S CHEESE, RED ONION & CHIVE FOCACCIA

If you are seeking the kind of comfort that carbs give you, you need not look any further.

SERVES 8–10

500g/1lb 2oz strong white
    bread flour, plus extra
    to dust
2 × 7g sachets of fast-action
    yeast
2 tsp sea salt
3 tbsp chopped chives
275ml/9fl oz lukewarm water
60ml/generous 2fl oz extra
    virgin olive oil
1 red onion, thickly sliced
1 tsp caster sugar
1 tbsp olive oil, plus 1 tsp
    to grease
150g/5oz soft goat's cheese
    log, crumbled
leaves stripped from
    2–3 sprigs of rosemary
1 tbsp olive oil

This springy bread, enriched with grassy olive oil and topped with creamy cheese and herbs, is like a blanket to wrap around yourself in the face of cold, disciplined diets. For best results, cut into wedges and eat while it is still warm.

Begin by sifting together the flour, yeast and 1 teaspoon of salt into a large mixing bowl. Throw in the chives and stir, then pour in the water and half the extra virgin olive oil. Bring the mixture together with your hands, then turn out onto a floured surface and knead until you have a springy, elastic dough. Cover with a damp tea towel and leave in a warm place for 45 minutes to rise – it should double in size.

Meanwhile, fry the onion and sugar in 1 tablespoon of the olive oil until the onions have caramelised. Set aside to cool.

Grease a 30cm/12in baking tin with the remaining 1 teaspoon of olive oil. Punch the air out of the dough, then push it down into the tin and leave to rise again for another 30 minutes.

Preheat the oven to 230°C/450°F/gas 8. Punch dimples into the surface of the dough with your fingertips and scatter on the onions, goat's cheese, rosemary and a final smattering of sea salt. Drizzle with the remaining extra virgin olive oil and bake in the oven for 15–20 minutes until crusty on the top and meltingly doughy on the inside.

LEMON, ASPARAGUS & PRAWN LINGUINE

There is no other pasta dish that evokes memories of long hot summers better than this one.

SERVES 4

350g/12oz dried linguine
2 bunches of fine asparagus
4 tsp olive oil
60g/2¼oz unsalted butter
3 garlic cloves, chopped
1 red chilli (deseeded if you
    don't want it too spicy),
    sliced
zest and juice of 1 lemon
1kg/2¼lb raw tiger prawns,
    peeled and deveined
sea salt and freshly ground
    black pepper
freshly grated Parmesan
    cheese, to serve

When handed lemons, some people make lemonade, but I like nothing more than to knock up this stunning sunny pasta. It's perfectly balanced, with flecks of chilli and zest, and seasonal pencil-thin asparagus. Added to this, the discovery of juicy prawns, hidden like coral jewels amongst the tangle of linguine, makes you feel like you're living, if not eating, la dolce vita.

Cook the pasta in plenty of boiling salted water until al dente. Strain it, reserving about 2 tablespoons of the cooking water.

Blanch the asparagus in boiling water until it is tender – 2–3 minutes. Drain and refresh in ice-cold water to prevent the retained heat from cooking it any further, then drain again.

Heat the olive oil in a pan, then melt in the butter. Add the garlic, chilli and lemon zest and cook for 1 minute until your kitchen is filled with its aroma. Tumble in the prawns and cook until they turn pink, then pour in the lemon juice, reserved water and seasoning to taste and shake over the heat to combine. Toss the cooked pasta and asparagus into the sauce and eat at once with a generous spoonful of Parmesan cheese.

TAGLIATELLE WITH ROASTED GARLIC, BACON & CHESTNUT MUSHROOMS

This pasta dish is the kind of supper you want to come home to after a challenging day at work.

Woody mushrooms, oozingly sweet roasted garlic, and crispy bacon in a cream sauce are the foody way of letting you know tomorrow will be a better day.

Preheat the oven to 200°C/400°F/gas 6. Slice the tops of the garlic bulbs and drizzle with a little of the olive oil. Wrap them in kitchen foil, put on a baking sheet and roast for 30 minutes. Leave to cool slightly.

Cook the pasta in boiling salted water until al dente. Drain.

Heat the remaining olive oil in a frying pan and fry the pancetta or bacon until it is golden, then add the mushrooms and cook again until they are golden brown. Throw in the chopped garlic and fry again for 2 minutes.

Squeeze the roasted garlic cloves to extract the pulp from each clove – it should ooze out quite easily. Stir the pulp into the mushroom mixture and, after 1 minute, stir in the cream and seasoning. Toss the cooked pasta in the sauce and serve immediately with a little Parmesan cheese.

SERVES 4

2 whole bulbs of garlic, plus
   2 extra cloves, chopped
2 tbsp olive oil
350g/12oz dried tagliatelle
100g/3½oz pancetta or
   rindless streaky bacon,
   cubed
300g/10oz chestnut
   mushrooms, sliced
150ml/5fl oz double cream
sea salt and freshly ground
   black pepper
freshly grated Parmesan
   cheese, to serve

CHAPTER TWO

Working it 9–5

Work to live, live to eat

Whether it's your wardrobe (vintage dress taken up an extra couple of inches) or your hair (choppy bob, dyed red) you like to put your own spin on things. So I'm guessing that when it comes to lunch, a prepackaged dried-out tuna sandwich isn't going to rock your yacht.

Canteen lunches are yawn-some – at most you'll get a soggy sandwich or a watered-down soup. And the last time you ventured out, all you came back with were a few pieces of questionable sushi and a considerably lighter purse. And don't even get me started on the sandwich delis – WHY, WHY, WHY! after a year of telling them you're on a diet, can they not hold the freakin' mayo...?

Dust down that lunchbox and take control. Home-made lunches are the healthier, cheaper and tastier option – a credible girl's edibles. Work can be repetitive, but your lunch needn't be – a packed lunch guarantees you something fresh and customised to your taste daily. You'll be rushing into work just to tuck in!

PASTA, CHORIZO & BEAN SOUP

Your payslip may sometimes feel unsatisfying – but your soup needn't be.

MAKES 2 LARGE SERVINGS

1 tbsp olive oil
50g/2oz uncooked chorizo
    sausage, chopped
    (see Kitchen-ade)
1 garlic clove, finely chopped
1 small red onion, finely
    chopped
1 celery stick, roughly
    chopped
leaves stripped from 1 small
    sprig of rosemary,
    chopped (optional)
200ml/7fl oz passata
400ml/14fl oz chicken stock
150g/5oz tinned cannellini
    beans, drained and rinsed
30g/generous 1oz dried pasta

This one is choc-full of big flavours and really has bite. As it cooks, the chorizo sausage seeps its smoky paprika fat into the base of the soup, tingeing it with a sunset stain. It's just the thing to put the fire back in your belly – you'll be demanding a pay rise in no time.

Heat the olive oil in a pan and fry the sausage until it's a little crisp and its paprika fat has run into the oil. Toss in the garlic, onion and celery and sauté until the onion is translucent. If you like, add a little chopped rosemary and then fry again for a few seconds.

Pour in the passata and chicken stock and tumble in the beans. Bring to the boil, then cover and simmer for 5 minutes. Add the pasta and cook until the pasta is tender but still al dente – about 10 minutes. If you're taking it to the office, pour into a vacuum flask to keep it warm.

KITCHEN-ADE
There are two types of chorizo sausage – the firmer ones with the tough skin are cured and ready to eat, but the ones best for frying and stews are the uncooked variety. They have a thin membrane and the squishiness of a regular sausage.

LEMON & SPINACH LENTIL SOUP

This soup is so wonderfully mealy and nourishing you don't even need bread to dip into it.

With the iron from the spinach and the protein-rich lentils, you'll be left fighting fit for an afternoon of good hard work.

Rinse the lentils until the water runs clear, then put them into a saucepan with the water, butter and a generous amount of seasoning. Bring to the boil, then cover the pan and simmer until the lentils are tender and creamy. This should take about 20 minutes.

Heat the olive oil in a frying pan, then sweat the onion and garlic until soft. Add the lemon zest and fry for another minute.

Once the lentils are tender, scoop the onions and garlic into the pan and rip in shreds of spinach – they'll take seconds to wilt. Squeeze in the lemon juice and take off the heat. Pour into a vacuum flask to keep it warm for the office and enjoy the fruits of your labour.

MAKES 4 SATISFYING BOWLFULS

225g/8oz split red lentils
1.5 litres/2½ pints water
1 knob of unsalted butter
sea salt and freshly ground
    black pepper to taste
2 tbsp olive oil
1 medium onion, chopped
4 garlic cloves, chopped
zest and juice of 1 lemon
100g/3½oz baby leaf
    spinach

RICE, GINGER & SESAME SWEETCORN BROTH

This mellow, sunshine-yellow soup is the perfect antidote to blue and manic Mondays, and it's such a cinch to prepare that the question of mania just doesn't arise.

MAKES 2 LARGE SERVINGS

1 tsp olive oil
200g/7oz tinned sweetcorn, drained
zest and juice of ½ lemon
¼ tsp turmeric
1 tsp grated fresh root ginger
500ml/17fl oz hot chicken stock
40g/1½oz basmati rice
a few drops of sesame oil
1 tbsp chopped fresh coriander

Heat the olive oil in a saucepan and then toss in the sweetcorn and lemon zest. Stir to coat with the oil and cook for 3 minutes, then sprinkle in the turmeric and ginger and stir-fry over a medium heat for a further 2 minutes.

Pour in the hot stock and drop in the rice. Bring to the boil, then cook over a low to medium heat for about 15 minutes or until the rice is tender. Squeeze in the lemon juice and sprinkle in a few drops of sesame oil. Top with the chopped coriander. (Pour into a vacuum flask to keep it warm for the office, if necessary.)

Preserved lemons

These have crept into the British taste consciousness and are available now in most supermarkets, but I sometimes like to make my own. It couldn't be simpler. Make cross slits vertically in a few unwaxed lemons, but don't slice all the way through – they still need to be joined at the bottom. Sterilise a pickling jar with boiling water and then fill it with as many lemons as you can squeeze in – I normally manage 10 – along with 6 peeled garlic cloves, a few cloves, a curl of cinnamon, a couple of whole red chillies and a 5cm/2in knob of peeled fresh root ginger. Top with white wine vinegar or cider vinegar. Close the jar tightly and store it in a cool dark place for 3–4 weeks for the lemons to mature. Their skins will become meltingly soft, and they will have picked up all the flavours of the ingredients in the vinegar.

TUNA & CHICKPEA SALAD
WITH PRESERVED LEMON & HARISSA DRESSING

You already have a hideous amount of demands on your time, so your lunch shouldn't be one of them.

Your inbox is pinging every few seconds, your phone is ringing off the hook and your in-tray is piled so high that your only view is of paper city...

This salad takes no more than 10 minutes to throw together and, because the ingredients come straight from your storecupboard, you don't even have to shop for it. Plus, it takes only about 2 minutes 37 seconds to chomp through, leaving you all the more time to plough through the expenses you've been procrastinating over. Talk about crunching figures!

Mix together the tuna, chickpeas, tomatoes, pickled lemon, olives and coriander. Heat a dry pan and toast the cumin until it is aromatic. Tip it into a pestle and mortar and crack with a few hefty hits. Sprinkle it over the tuna mix.

In a bowl, whisk together the harissa, lemon juice and extra virgin olive oil and season to taste. Dress the tuna salad.

MAKES 2 SERVINGS

200g/7oz tinned tuna in
   olive oil, drained
1 × 400g tin of chickpeas,
   drained and rinsed
10 cherry tomatoes, halved
1 small preserved or pickled
   lemon, finely chopped
   (see page 55)
10 of your favourite olives –
   I like to use green ones
   as big as grapes here
2 heaped tbsp roughly
   chopped fresh coriander
½ tsp cumin seeds

For the dressing
1 tsp harissa paste
   (see page 42)
juice of ½ lemon
3 tbsp extra virgin olive oil
sea salt and freshly ground
   black pepper

COUSCOUS & ROASTED VEGETABLE SALAD
WITH POMEGRANATE MOLASSES DRESSING

When it comes to packed lunches you can't get more convenient than this.

Couscous is so simple – it virtually cooks itself, and the roasted vegetables are a complete no-brainer. The addition of the astringently sour pomegranate molasses dressing really lifts the salad, and your spirits – just the lunchtime tonic for an overworked soul.

**MAKES ENOUGH FOR
2 LARGE HELPINGS**

1 small courgette, trimmed and cut into
   large chunks
1 small aubergine, trimmed and cut into
   large chunks
1 small red pepper, deseeded and cut
   into large chunks
2 red onions, sliced into thick wedges
1 small fennel bulb, sliced into thick
   wedges
1 tbsp extra virgin olive oil
1 tsp coriander seeds, crushed
12 cherry tomatoes

200g/7oz couscous
350ml/12fl oz chicken or vegetable
   stock
a little unsalted butter or olive oil
   (optional)
2 handfuls of baby leaf spinach
sea salt and freshly ground black
   pepper

For the dressing

2 tbsp pomegranate molasses
   (see Kitchen-ade)
3 tbsp olive oil
1 tbsp water
½ tsp caster sugar

Preheat the oven to 200°C/400°F/gas 6. Toss the courgette, aubergine, red pepper, onions and fennel in a roasting tray with extra virgin olive oil and then sprinkle with the coriander seeds and seasoning, making sure everything gets an even dousing of oil and spice. Roast the vegetables in the oven for 30 minutes, then add the tomatoes and cook for a further 10 minutes, turning the vegetables a few times while they are cooking. Remove from the oven and leave to cool.

Put the couscous into a large heatproof bowl and pour the chicken or vegetable stock over it (or you can use plain hot water if you prefer). Stir well, cover with a plate and leave for 10 minutes for the water to be absorbed. Fluff up with a fork and leave to cool. You can add a touch of butter or olive oil to the grains at this stage if you wish.

Whisk together the dressing ingredients in a bowl – the water should help to loosen up the molasses, which can often be thick and treacly.

Add the spinach to the vegetables and then mix with the couscous in a large bowl. Pour the dressing over and let it steep until you are ready to eat. I have to admit, being as delicious as it is, this often becomes an 11.00am snack and hardly makes it to lunch.

KITCHEN-ADE

Pomegranate molasses are made by boiling down the juice of pomegranates until it is dark and syrupy. It is both sweet and intensely sour and is used in sauces and dressings, a little like tamarind and thick balsamic vinegar. It keeps in its bottle indefinitely and is an essential ingredient for the modern storecupboard. Buy it in your local Middle Eastern supermarket – I go to my favourite one, Persepolis in Brixton, to stock up on it and other Persian goodies.

TUNA SASHIMI WITH AVOCADO SALAD

This dish is low on effort, but high in taste – it takes no more than 10 minutes to throw together.

SERVES 2

1 tbsp olive oil
½ tsp sesame oil
1 tbsp light soy sauce
1 tbsp rice vinegar
a dot of wasabi
175g/6oz fillet of fresh tuna,
    cut into thin slices

For the salad

1 avocado, sliced
8 cherry tomatoes, halved
2 heaped tbsp freshly torn
    coriander
3 spring onions, sliced
juice of 1 lime
sea salt and freshly ground
    black pepper
1 tsp toasted sesame seeds,
    to garnish

Even without the tuna the salad is just delicious, but the tuna makes it more substantial. I always pack it in a lunchbox with an icepack compartment to ensure the tuna stays as fresh as possible.

Pour the olive oil, sesame oil, soy sauce and rice vinegar into a dish and then whisk in the wasabi. Add the tuna and make sure it is well coated.

To assemble the salad, layer the avocado, tomatoes, coriander and spring onions, then squeeze the lime juice over and season to taste. Top with the dressed tuna and a sprinkling of sesame seeds. It certainly beats a soggy sandwich!

KITCHEN-ADE

When buying tuna to eat raw, it is best to ask your fishmonger if it is sushi grade. This simply means that when it is caught, it is frozen at an icy temperature for seven days and then stored at a temperature of -20°C. This process kills off any harmful parasites or bacteria.

To test the freshness of the fish, follow my three golden rules:

1   Follow your nose – if it smells fishy, don't buy it. It should have a neutral aroma.
2   The colour of fresh tuna should be beautifully opaque and even – tuna ranges from blush pink to deep red depending on the species.
3   Touch it – it should be firm yet yielding; if it's as tough as old boots, walk away.

PEANUT BUTTER, NOODLE & CHICKEN SALAD

If you like eating peanut butter with more than just jelly and two slices of white, you'll love this crunchily addictive salad. It's packed with good-for-you raw vegetables, lean chicken and, of course, a whole load of peanut butter. A true power lunch.

SERVES 1

100g/3½oz rice noodles
½ red pepper, deseeded and
    cut into thin strips
1 small carrot, cut into thin
    strips
1 celery stick, cut into thin
    strips
1 handful of spinach,
    shredded
1 spring onion, chopped
50g/2oz beansprouts
1 hard-boiled egg
100g/3½oz lean cooked
    chicken fillets

For the dressing

3 tbsp peanut butter
    (see Kitchen-ade)
2 tbsp light soy sauce
juice of ½ lime
1 tsp honey
1 tbsp rice vinegar
1 tsp grated fresh root ginger
1 garlic clove, crushed
½ red chilli, deseeded and
    chopped

Boil the noodles in plenty of salted water for 3 minutes, then drain and plunge them into ice-cold water to stop them cooking any more. Drain again and put into a large salad bowl along with the red pepper, carrot, celery, spinach, spring onion and beansprouts. Toss well, making sure the vegetables are evenly spread through the net of noodles.

To make the dressing, combine the peanut butter with the soy sauce, lime juice, honey and rice vinegar. Stir in the ginger, garlic and chilli. Pour the dressing over the salad and then top with the hard-boiled egg and chicken.

KITCHEN-ADE

Choose an unsweetened natural peanut butter for this dressing. Whole Earth do a fantastic one that is readily available in most supermarkets.

SOY SESAME CHICKEN STICKS WITH NUTTY COLESLAW

If the juiciest thing in your office is the gossip, you need to get a real lunch.

These succulent chicken sticks pack in a heap of oriental flavour, while the coleslaw comes with a healthier-than-mayo nutty twist. And psst, rumour has it it's really easy to do, too.

To make the coleslaw, combine the carrot, cabbage, spring onions and coriander. Whisk the peanut butter, rice vinegar, soy sauce and lime juice together to make the dressing, then toss through the salad.

Make a marinade for the chicken by whisking together the rice vinegar, soy sauce, sesame oil, honey, chilli and sesame seeds. Pour over the chicken and leave to marinate for at least 1 hour. Meanwhile, soak some wooden skewers in water to stop them burning.

When you are ready to cook, preheat the grill to hot. Thread the chicken onto the skewers and grill for 10 minutes, turning the skewers to cook the chicken evenly. Serve hot or cold with the coleslaw.

SERVES 2

1 tsp rice vinegar
1 tbsp light soy sauce
1 tsp sesame oil
2 tbsp honey
1 red chilli (deseeded if you don't want it too spicy), chopped
1 tbsp sesame seeds
200g/7oz skinned, boned chicken thighs, diced into 3cm/1¼in pieces

For the coleslaw

1 small carrot, grated
100g/3½oz shredded white cabbage
2 spring onions, finely chopped
1 heaped tbsp chopped fresh coriander
1 heaped tbsp smooth unsweetened natural peanut butter (see page 62)
1 tsp rice vinegar
2 tsp light soy sauce
2 tbsp lime juice

PLOUGHMAN'S PASTIES

Cheese and pickle is a national treasure so it shouldn't just be reserved for smearing between doorsteps of white bread. I like to use mature cheddar for a tantalising tang.

MAKES 8

1 onion, finely chopped
250g/9oz Cheddar cheese,
    grated
5 tbsp pickle
500g/1lb 2oz ready-to-roll
    all-butter shortcrust
    pastry
plain flour, to dust
2 eggs, beaten

Preheat the oven to 180°C/350°F/gas 4. Mix the onion with the cheese and pickle in a large mixing bowl.

Roll out the pastry on a well-floured surface until it is 5mm/¼in thick. Cut out eight saucer-sized circles from it. Divide the filling between the circles, leaving a 5mm/¼in border around the edge. Dampen the edge of each circle with a little water and gather up the edges to meet at the top of the filling. Crimp the edges firmly together.

Place the pasties on a baking sheet and brush with beaten egg. Bake for 25 minutes until the pastry is golden and cooked through. Enjoy these hot or cold.

SALMON SUSHI FINGER SANDWICHES

Abandon the bread bin and knock up your very own sushi sandwich.

MAKES 6 FINGER SANDWICHES

175g/6oz sushi rice
225ml/7½fl oz water
1 tbsp caster sugar
1½ tbsp rice vinegar
½ tsp sea salt
1 sheet of nori
2–3 slices of smoked salmon
2 tsp capers
2 tsp pickled ginger
a few thin slices of
    cucumber, cut lengthways
1 tsp black sesame seeds
soy sauce, to serve

Don't panic – you don't need the samurai skills of a Japanese masterchef here – it really is as easy as making a sarnie. Once you've cooked the rice (which, by the way, isn't as tricky as it may seem), all you've got to do is flatten it out like bread and fill it. No complicated rolling, chopping, or chopsticks required here – just easy peasy Japanesey.

Wash the rice in several changes of cold water until the water runs clear. Put the rice into a saucepan with the water and bring to the boil. Once it reaches boiling point, turn down the heat to low, cover the pan with a tight lid and cook until the rice is tender and the water has been absorbed. Turn off the heat and let the rice sit, still covered, to steam for 10 minutes.

Meanwhile, combine the sugar, rice vinegar and salt in a small pan and heat over a low flame until the sugar and salt have dissolved. Pour into a bowl to cool.

Spread the rice out over a plate, sprinkle the cooled rice vinegar seasoning over it and mix with a wooden paddle. Leave the rice to cool.

Line a rectangular mould (I use the cartons you get Chinese takeaway in or a small rectangular sandwich box) with a piece of cling film large enough to hang over the sides of it. Using a pair of scissors, snip a piece of nori large enough to cover the base and place in the mould. Spoon half the cooled rice over the nori, flattening and pressing it down as you go. When it is smooth and flattened, top with the salmon, capers, pickled ginger and cucumber and sprinkle with the sesame seeds. Spoon the rest of the rice over the filling and flatten at the top to create a sandwich. Top with a slice of nori large enough to cover the top.

Pull out the cling film carefully to unmould the sandwich and then cut with a wet knife into 5 or 6 slices. Eat dipped in soy with a dot of wasbi.

KITCHEN-ADE

I have used salmon here, but you can use a whole host of ingredients from tuna and pickled radishes to grilled tofu and carrot and cooked chicken.

CHAPTER THREE

Comfort food

When you've got no one to give you a hug, you need a hug on a plate

There's something about good old home cooking that always seems to make your blues take a hike. Take, for example, chicken soup, also known as Jewish penicillin; science bods have proved that it does, in fact, have properties that say boo to the 'flu. As if we needed proof!

Or then there's the warm and fuzzy feeling that only tucking into a traditional shepherd's pie can give you. How can you possibly have a care in the world when there's a dish full of creamy all-butter mash to be forked up? Pour out a serving of my chicken noodle soup and I promise both the golden colour and satisfying taste will soothe your soul. Or serve yourself a generous ladle of rice pudding and it's like finding solace in your mother's lap.

Now, turn that frown upside-down, grab a fork and indulge in the very best of comfort eating. After all, there's no place like home cooking!

LEEK, POTATO & BACON SOUP

The chemistry of leeks and potatoes may not be an explosive one, but when you are after a bit of a pick-me-up it's familiarity you seek.

SERVES 6

1 litre/1¾ pints good-quality
    chicken stock
1 large floury potato, diced
150g/5oz pancetta, diced
1 generous tbsp olive oil
2 hefty leeks, trimmed and
    chopped
2 garlic cloves, chopped
60ml/generous 2fl oz single
    cream
300ml/10fl oz full-fat milk
freshly ground nutmeg
sea salt and freshly ground
    black pepper

Leeks and potatoes are like the couple on a pier who've grown old together, a cliché, but a heart-warming one all the same.

Bring the stock to the boil, then add the potato and simmer until tender – 10–12 minutes.

Meanwhile, pan-fry the pancetta in the olive oil until it is cooked and golden. Remove from the pan with a slotted spoon and drain on kitchen paper. Sauté the leeks and garlic in the bacon fat until they are soft but still pale.

Stir the leeks and garlic, cream, milk, pancetta, nutmeg and seasoning into the stock and then liquidise in batches until it is velvet smooth. Eat yourself to contentment.

CHINESE CHICKEN NOODLE SOUP

When it's freezing outside, you need something that's going to really warm your bones.

The heavy hit of ginger in this soup will not only make you feel toasty on the inside, its clean, golden broth is guaranteed to give you back your chi. Perfect chow for the chilly weather blues.

Put the garlic and ginger into a food processor and blitz to a fine paste. Mix it with the chicken, chilli, soy sauce and rice wine in a bowl. Add 1 tablespoon of the sesame oil, the rice wine vinegar and sugar and leave to marinate for 30 minutes.

In a pan, heat 1 tablespoon of sesame oil and fry the carrot and spring onions for 2–3 minutes. Pour in the stock and bring to the boil. Once it's boiling, add the chicken, cover the pan and simmer for about 20 minutes or until the chicken is cooked through.

Now add the noodles and pak choi and simmer again for 3–4 minutes until the noodles are cooked. Scatter with fresh coriander and slurp away your winter blues.

SERVES 4

3 garlic cloves, roughly chopped

2.5cm/1in knob of fresh root ginger, peeled and roughly chopped

225g/8oz skinned, boned chicken thighs, cut into thin strips

1 long red chilli (deseeded if you don't want it too spicy), finely shredded

2 tbsp light soy sauce

2 tbsp rice wine (mirin)

2 tbsp sesame oil

1 tbsp rice wine vinegar

1½ tsp caster sugar

1 carrot, thinly sliced on the diagonal

6 spring onions, chopped

1 litre/1¾ pints chicken stock

30g/generous 1oz rice noodles

2 pak choi leaves, roughly torn and stalks chopped

5 tbsp chopped fresh coriander

ROASTED TOMATO SOUP

WITH HAM & CHEESE SOLDIERS

Friends and lovers may come and go, but there is nothing as constant as a deep bowl of titian tomato soup.

SERVES 6

1kg/2¼lb ripe tomatoes, halved
4 garlic cloves, chopped
3 bushy sprigs of thyme
2 red onions, sliced
sea salt and freshly ground black pepper
1 tbsp caster sugar
1 tbsp olive oil
2 tbsp balsamic vinegar
1 litre/1¾ pints good-quality vegetable
    stock
fresh basil leaves and double cream or
    crème fraîche, to serve

Whether it's home-made or poured straight from a tin, tomato soup is the age-old medicine to lift the failing spirit. This one has plenty of garlic in it to stave off a cold, and the tomatoes are roasted for a concentrated, robust flavour. Plainly speaking, it's cosy in a cup.

Preheat the oven to 220°C/425°F/gas 7. Arrange the tomatoes in a roasting tin, cut-side up. Strew them with the garlic, thyme, onions and seasoning to taste, then sprinkle with the sugar. Drizzle the olive oil and balsamic vinegar over and roast for 25–30 minutes until the tomatoes are blistered. Remove from the oven.

Bring the stock up to the boil, then add the tomatoes, garlic and onions. Cook for 5 minutes, mushing the tomatoes up with the back of a wooden spoon. Pour into a blender and liquidise until you have a glossy smooth soup. Serve topped with some fresh basil and a swirl of cream or dollop of crème fraîche, accompanied by the soldiers.

To make the ham and cheese soldiers, heat a griddle pan until very hot. Brush the melted butter over one side of each slice of bread. Spread mustard over the unbuttered sides of 6 slices and then layer with the cheese and ham. Top with the remaining bread, butter-side up, and then griddle on both sides until crisp and golden. Cut each sandwich into 4 soldiers. Serve with the soup.

For the ham and cheese soldiers

60g/2¼oz melted unsalted butter

12 slices of thick white toasting bread

3–4 heaped tbsp English mustard

250g/9oz Gruyère cheese

12 slices of wafer-thin smoked ham

CAULIFLOWER & BROCCOLI CHEESE
WITH TOMATO SAUCE & PARMESAN BREADCRUMBS

Cauliflower cheese is one of those foods that you despise as a child and get nostalgic about in more mature years.

SERVES 6

1 medium cauliflower, cut
    into florets
1 medium head of broccoli,
    cut into florets
½ lemon (optional)
70g/2¾oz Gruyère
    cheese

For the cheese sauce
40g/1½oz unsalted butter
40g/1½oz plain flour
600ml/1 pint full-fat milk
70g/2¾oz Cheddar or
    Gruyère cheese
sprinkling of freshly ground
    nutmeg
sea salt and freshly ground
    black pepper

My yearning for cauliflower cheese doesn't quite stretch to the greying florets dipped in a processed cheese sauce we were served at school. This sophisticated deconstructed version is cooked in a velvet cheese sauce, with a side of zesty tomato sauce and Parmesan breadcrumbs.

Bring a large pan of water to the boil and plunge in the cauliflower. Simmer for about 6 minutes, then add the broccoli and cook for a further 4 minutes or until both vegetables are tender. (Adding half a lemon to the boiling water will stop the broccoli and cauliflower from discolouring.) Drain well and set aside.

To make the tomato sauce, fry the onion and garlic in a little olive oil until soft and golden. Throw in the lemon zest and chilli and fry again for a further 2 minutes, then stir in the tomatoes, sugar and lemon juice. Let the sauce cook slowly on a low heat for about 20 minutes. Once it's stewed to a jammy consistency, season and sprinkle in the oregano and basil.

Preheat the oven to 200°C/400°F/gas 6. Make the cheese sauce. Melt the butter in a saucepan and, when it's foaming, whisk in the flour. Cook for 30 seconds and then pour in the milk, a little at a time, whisking it to stop the sauce going lumpy. Once all the milk has gone in, bring the sauce to the boil, then turn down the heat and simmer until it has thickened slightly, stirring continuously. Stir in the Cheddar or Gruyère cheese, nutmeg and seasoning and simmer again, stirring, for 2 minutes. Remove from the heat.

Arrange the cauliflower and broccoli in a baking dish and pour the cheese sauce over. Top with the Gruyère cheese and bake in the oven for 20 minutes until it's crisp and golden on top.

To make the breadcrumbs, melt the butter in a heavy-based pan until foaming. Sprinkle in the breadcrumbs and sauté until they begin to go crisp and golden, then add the Parmesan. Turn off the heat and stir.

Serve the cauliflower cheese topped with the breadcrumbs and a dollop of warm tomato sauce.

For the tomato sauce

1 red onion, chopped
2 garlic cloves, chopped
a slug of olive oil
zest and juice of 1 lemon
1 dried red chilli, broken into
    pieces
1 × 400g tin of chopped
    tomatoes
1 tsp caster sugar
1 tsp dried oregano
8–10 fresh basil leaves,
    roughly torn

**For the Parmesan
breadcrumbs**

1 large knob of unsalted
    butter
100g/3½oz breadcrumbs
    made
    from stale ciabatta
40g/1½oz grated Parmesan
    cheese

COCK-A-LEEKIE PIE

If I am completely honest, I'll eat anything wrapped in pastry like my career depends on it.

SERVES 6

8 chicken thighs, skinned, boned and chopped into bite-sized chunks
sea salt and freshly ground black pepper
1 large knob of unsalted butter
2 leeks, trimmed and chopped into thick chunks
250g/9oz chestnut mushrooms, halved
leaves stripped from 4 bushy sprigs of thyme
zest and juice of 1 lemon
2 tbsp plain flour, plus extra to dust
1 glass of white wine
200ml/7fl oz double cream
3 tbsp chopped fresh flat-leaf parsley
375g/13oz ready-made puff pastry
1 egg beaten

Flaky, shortcrust, savoury or sweet, I'm not terribly fussy – I'm just a crustafarian. This hearty pie, deep as sleep, relights my fire when I'm feeling burnt out. The tender morsels of chicken in a thick cream sauce, topped with crumbly pastry, make a pie with an instant high.

Preheat the oven to 200°C/400°F/gas 6. Season the chicken generously with salt and pepper. Melt the butter in a pan, toss in the chicken and cook until it is sealed on all sides, then add the leeks, mushrooms, thyme and lemon zest. Once the mushrooms are nutty and brown, sprinkle in the flour and keep stirring for a minute or so, then pour in the wine. When the wine has almost evaporated, pour in the cream and lemon juice, mix and simmer for 5 minutes. Stir in the parsley. Turn the mixture into a large pie dish and leave to cool.

Roll out the pastry on a lightly floured surface until 1cm/½in thick and then drape over the pie dish. Carefully cut away any excess pastry and then go around the edge of the pie dish pressing down with a fork so it is well sealed. Brush the beaten egg all over the surface of the pastry for a golden glaze and bake in the oven for 25 minutes until the pastry is well browned.

Serve with mashed potato for the ultimate hug on a plate.

PANKO PARMESAN CHICKEN

This breaded chicken really is nursery food for adults. You can use ordinary breadcrumbs, but I urge you to seek out panko breadcrumbs from an oriental foodstore – they give it an off-the-Richter crunch.

SERVES 4

5 tbsp olive oil
4 chicken breasts, skinned and boned
3 large eggs
3 tbsp Dijon mustard
150g/5oz panko breadcrumbs
100g/3½oz freshly grated Parmesan cheese
sea salt and freshly ground black pepper

For the buttered cabbage
50g/2oz unsalted butter
1 Savoy cabbage, core removed and shredded
generous grating of fresh nutmeg

Preheat the oven to 200°C/400°F/gas 6. Grease a baking sheet with 1 tablespoon of olive oil.

Next, butterfly the chicken breasts, so you have 8 thin slices of meat – lay them flat on a board and, using a sharp knife, cut horizontally through the breast, but not all the way through. Open them out. Cutting them open in this way means they will cook faster and more evenly.

Beat the eggs with the mustard in a shallow bowl. In another bowl, mix the breadcrumbs with the Parmesan and seasoning.

Dip each piece of chicken in the beaten eggs and then turn in the breadcrumbs to coat well. Repeat to give a double layer of breadcrumbs – this will give extra crunch. Lay the coated chicken breasts on the baking sheet and drizzle with the remaining olive oil. Bake for 20 minutes, turning them over halfway through the cooking time, until they are crisp, golden and cooked through.

To make the cabbage, melt the butter in a pan and then sauté the cabbage for 10 minutes until softened but still crisp. Season with salt and pepper and a generous grating of nutmeg. Serve with the chicken.

CRISPY WHITEBAIT WITH A QUICK TARTARE SAUCE

I first ate deep-fried whitebait at The Chelsea Kitchen, a great British establishment that is now very sadly RIP.

It came piled high still hissing from the hot oil, served with a wedge of lemon and a small bowl of tartare sauce. I nibbled my first plateful dodging the heads of the little small fry, but by my second helping any such *Finding Nemo* sympathies had flown out of the window – I devoured them whole, unable to waste a single morsel. I have spiced up my home-made version with a little toasted cumin, which provides a contrasting heat against the cooling tartare sauce. One bite and you too will be hooked.

Preparing the tartare sauce is easy: just mix all the ingredients together – it really is no more complicated than that.

Heat the groundnut oil in a deep-fat fryer.

Dry-roast the cumin in a hot frying pan. As soon as it begins to pop, take it off the heat, place in a pestle and mortar with the sea salt and crush into a coarse powder. Mix the cumin-salt in with the flour and cayenne pepper and then throw in the fish and coat well.

Shake off the excess flour from the fish and deep-fry in batches. They should take 2 minutes to crisp up nicely. Be patient – don't overcrowd the pan or you'll end up with a soggy mess. Drain on kitchen paper and then serve immediately with the tartare sauce, a wedge of lime and some bread and butter.

KITCHEN-ADE
There are some excellent varieties of frozen whitebait available if you can't get hold of any fresh.

SERVES 2 TO SHARE

groundnut oil for deep-frying
   (see Cook's Notes, page 12)
1 tsp cumin seeds
1 tsp sea salt
125g/4oz plain flour
½ tsp cayenne pepper
500g/1lb 2oz whitebait,
   rinsed and patted dry
lime wedges, to serve
bread and butter, to serve

For the tartare sauce
100g/3½oz good-quality mayonnaise
2 tbsp capers, roughly chopped
2 tbsp cornichons, roughly chopped
1 tbsp chopped flat-leaf parsley
1 tbsp chopped fresh dill
juice of ½ lemon
sea salt and freshly ground black pepper

MOZZARELLA & BASIL-STUFFED MEATBALLS IN TOMATO & CHIANTI SAUCE

A tasty meatball should be rolled from mince with a good fat content, which is why I prefer succulent pink pork mince speckled with nuggets of fat.

SERVES 4

1 medium onion, chopped
vegetable oil for frying
2 garlic cloves, chopped
500g/1lb 2oz pork mince
50g/2oz fresh white
　　breadcrumbs
1 tbsp fresh oregano
3 heaped tbsp chopped fresh
　　flat-leaf parsley
zest of 1 lemon
juice of ½ lemon
25g/1oz freshly grated
　　Parmesan cheese,
　　plus extra to serve
¼ tsp grated nutmeg
1 egg, lightly beaten
1 tsp hot paprika
100g/3½oz buffalo
　　mozzarella cheese
1 handful of torn fresh basil
　　leaves, plus extra to serve
sea salt and freshly ground
　　black pepper
cooked spaghetti, to serve

It should melt in the mouth – a stuffing of oozing mozzarella sees to that here – and, finally, it should have heat: I use a generous teaspoon of hot paprika or occasionally a fat red chilli. Great balls of fire – I think I've got it!

To make the meatballs, fry the onion in a little vegetable oil until soft and translucent, then add the garlic and fry for another 2 minutes. Leave to cool.

In a large bowl, combine the mince, breadcrumbs, oregano, parsley, lemon zest and juice, Parmesan, nutmeg, beaten egg, paprika and the cooled fried onion and garlic. Mix well.

Tear the mozzarella into 20 pieces and wrap each piece in a small basil leaf like you would wrap a sweetie. Shape the mince around the basil and mozzarella to make 20 small meatballs.

Heat a little vegetable oil in a frying pan. Carefully place the meatballs in the oil and brown them on all sides over a medium to low heat. Fry them in small batches, making sure you don't overcrowd the pan. Once they are golden brown and sealed, remove them from the pan and drain on kitchen paper.

Make the sauce. Drain the oil from the pan and heat the olive oil. Once it is hot, sauté the onion over a medium heat until soft. Add the garlic and chilli and cook for a further 2 minutes. Next, pour in the wine and bubble on a high heat, scraping up all the brown bits of flavour stuck to the pan. Cook until the wine has reduced by half, then stir in the tomatoes, parsley, sugar and seasoning. Bring the sauce up to the boil, then reduce the heat, return the meatballs to the pan and cover. Simmer for 25 minutes, until the meatballs are cooked through. Serve with spaghetti or any other pasta of your choice and top with fresh basil and Parmesan cheese.

KITCHEN-ADE

To really give the sauce a warming roundness, choose a full-bodied Chianti, and go easy on the spaghetti – too much and it'll turn into a plate of stodge.

For the Chianti and tomato sauce

2 tbsp olive oil
1 large onion, chopped
2 fat garlic cloves, chopped
1 dried red chilli, crumbled
250ml/8fl oz Chianti
2 × 400g tins of chopped tomatoes
3 heaped tbsp chopped fresh flat-leaf parsley
1 tsp caster sugar
sea salt and freshly ground black pepper

SPICY SHEPHERD'S PIE

This shepherd's pie is layered with a wall of mashed potato thick enough to insulate an igloo.

SERVES 4

generous slug of olive oil
1 onion, very finely chopped
1 carrot, chopped
3 garlic cloves, chopped
1 tsp cumin
½ tsp ground cinnamon
500g/1lb 2oz minced lamb
200ml/7fl oz chopped tomatoes
1 tbsp tomato purée
2.5cm/1in fresh root ginger
2 green chillies (deseeded if
    you don't want it too spicy),
    chopped
1 tbsp red wine vinegar
sea salt and freshly ground
    black pepper
100g/3½oz frozen peas
250ml/8fl oz boiling water
ketchup, to serve

FOR THE MASH

750g/1½lb floury potatoes, such
    as King Edwards, peeled
75g/3oz unsalted butter
2 egg yolks
40ml/1½fl oz full-fat milk
40ml/1½fl oz double cream
a light sprinkling of hot paprika

So if the temperature's taken a nosedive, and daylight's over before you've even switched off your 7.00am alarm, this is just the dish to warm body and soul. Think of it as a foodie anti-freeze. The extra spices and chilli will have you feeling toasty in no time.

Preheat the oven to 200°C/400°F/gas 6. Chop the potatoes for the mash into small cubes and simmer in a pan of salted water until tender – 10–15 minutes. Drain.

Meanwhile, heat the olive oil in a large pan and sauté the onion, carrot and garlic until they are soft and golden brown. Add the cumin and cinnamon and fry for a few minutes until they're beautifully fragrant. Add the mince and brown it off, breaking up any lumps with a wooden spoon.

Once the meat is well browned, pour in the tomatoes and tomato purée along with the ginger, chillies, vinegar and seasoning. Let the mixture bubble and cook for about 8 minutes. Once the tomatoes have broken down, tumble in the peas, stir well, and then pour in the water. Bring to the boil, then cover and simmer for 25 minutes.

Mash the potatoes, then beat in the butter and 2 egg yolks. Slowly pour in the milk and cream and mash again, ensuring you have a smooth, lump-free mash.

Pour the meat into an ovenproof dish and smother with the mash. Let some of it peak up – these bits will go lovely and crisp and help to make your shepherd's pie look rustic and home-made. Sprinkle with the paprika and bake in the oven for 25 minutes until bubbling and golden. Eat in front of the fire, plate balanced on your lap, with a dollop of ketchup.

CARDAMOM BISCUITS

Nothing spells comfort like a cup of tea and a biscuit to dunk into it.

MAKES 26 SMALL BISCUITS

100ml/3½fl oz vegetable oil, plus extra to grease
200g/7oz plain flour
50g/2oz gram flour or chickpea flour
75g/3oz icing sugar
½ tsp crushed cardamom seeds
14 pistachios, shelled and spilt in half lengthways

When I was growing up these were my absolute favourites. I just can't get enough of their crumbly texture and the warm spicy hug of the cardamom. They're good with a regular builder's brew, but to really make the most of them, dunk into a cup of Indian tea.

Preheat the oven to 180°C/350°F/gas 4 and grease a baking sheet.

Sift all the dry ingredients into a mixing bowl, add the vegetable oil and knead to a firm dough. Take heaped teaspoon-sized pieces of the dough and roll each one into a ball in the palm of your hand. Flatten into a disc and press a piece of pistachio into the centre of each one.

Place on the baking sheet and bake for about 25 minutes until the biscuits are golden brown. Leave to cool and firm on a wire rack.

CHEAT'S INDIAN TEA

This recipe cuts out all the pot-watching and makes an instant cup of chai that is every bit as good as the real McCoy.

Normally, Indian tea is a bit of a process. It's boiled with spices in a saucepan and brewed for an eternity, before the pouring in of a liberal amount of milk – only for it to boil over and spoil your lovely clean cooker the second your back is turned.

Boil the water in a kettle. While it's boiling, lightly bruise all the spices and pop into a teapot, along with the tea bags or loose tea. Pour the boiling water into the pot and let it brew for a few minutes. Pour into cups and add milk and sugar to your taste. A pot of bliss.

MAKES 4 SPICY CUPS

4 mugs of water
2 tsp fennel seeds
3 green cardamom pods
1 cinnamon stick
5 cloves
4 tea bags or 2 heaped
 teaspoons loose tea
 (I love Kenyan tea)
milk and sugar, to taste

OREO COOKIE CHEESECAKE

If there was one pudding I could dive into face-first it would be this one.

SERVES 12

For the base
250g/9oz Oreo cookies
50g/2oz unsalted butter,
   melted

For the topping
500g/1lb 2oz cream cheese
1 tbsp vanilla extract
4 large eggs, separated
100g/3½oz golden caster
   sugar
200g/7oz soured cream
200g/7oz Oreo cookies

There is nothing that quite compares to its dense pillowy texture and, where the biscuit is concerned, this one is a double hitter. It's sweet, but not overly so – which, like a lover who plays hard-to-get, just leaves you wanting even more.

Preheat the oven to 170°C/325°F/gas 3. To make the base, put your Oreo cookies into a freezer bag and bash with a rolling pin until they are smashed into fine smithereens. Mix with the melted butter and then press down firmly into a 20cm/8in springform cake tin. Bake for 15 minutes just to harden the crumb slightly and then leave to cool.

Now for that heavenly topping. Beat the cream cheese, vanilla extract, egg yolks and sugar together, add the soured cream and beat again. Crumble in the remaining Oreos and stir to make sure they are evenly spread through the mix.

Whisk the egg whites until they form soft peaks – this is what is going to give your cheesecake that wonderfully yielding texture. Carefully fold the egg whites into the cheese mixture, being careful not to knock out the air.

Pour the mixture over the cooled base and then bake for 1 hour 45 minutes. Don't be tempted to open the oven door, not even for a peek – good things come to those who wait! Once the cooking time is up and the cake is golden brown, turn off the oven. Open the oven door and leave the cake to sit in the oven for a further hour.

Serve cool. It's best eaten in bed, with a spoon like a spade.

KITCHEN-ADE
If you don't want to use Oreos, bourbons and custards creams also work well.

CARROT-SPICED RICE PUDDING

Carrot in rice pudding may sound looney, but I promise you don't have to be Bugs Bunny to appreciate it.

Once you've tried this, you'll never make it any other way again. The grated carrots break down in cooking and add their own natural sweetness to the pudding, while the cardamom adds a warming note of spice. That's all, folks.

Pour the milk into a heavy-based saucepan and stir in the rice and carrots. Simmer the ingredients over a low heat, stirring as you go, for 15–20 minutes. When the rice has completely cooked, add the sugar, almonds and cardamom seeds. Simmer again for a further 10 minutes, stirring until the sugar has completely dissolved.

Finally, pour in the cream and heat for another 2–3 minutes until the cream has imparted its satin texture throughout the pudding. Serve hot or cold.

SERVES 6

1.2 litres/2 pints full-fat milk

100g/3½oz pudding rice

2 medium carrots, peeled and grated

60g/2¼oz caster sugar

50g/2oz blanched almonds, peeled and chopped into fine slivers

1 tsp crushed cardamom seeds

200ml/7fl oz double cream

AFTERNOON TEA PUDDING

I wish there was more time to take afternoon tea.

A 3.00pm table of scones and celeb-spotting at the Wolseley is my idea of an afternoon well spent, but with everyone's hectic schedules and the Wolseley's infamous waiting list, the sad reality is we'd be lucky if we got a look-in with a packet of digestives. Thankfully, there is always time for an after-dinner pudding and here's one that makes up for what you missed at teatime.

SERVES 6

40g/1½oz unsalted butter, plus extra to grease
6 scones
raspberry jam
3 large eggs
125g/4oz caster sugar
250ml/8fl oz double cream
250ml/8fl oz full-fat milk
1 vanilla pod
clotted cream, to serve

Preheat the oven to 190°C/375°F/gas 5. Grease a baking dish with butter.

Slice the scones thinly (you should get about three slices from a regular-sized scone), spread butter and jam liberally on one side of each slice and start arranging in the dish, overlapping the scones as you go, jam face up. If you want to make individual portions, use small ramekins and layer in one scone per person, making sure the top layer is well covered with jam.

In a bowl, mix together the eggs and sugar until the sugar is well dissolved. Now, in a saucepan, heat the cream, milk and vanilla pod until simmering. Take off the heat, remove the vanilla pod and pour over the egg mixture, whisking to form a custard.

Pour the custard over the scones and leave to soak for about 15 minutes. Pop your dish into a roasting tin, pour boiling water into the tin to come halfway up the sides of the dish and bake in the oven for 40 minutes. Cooking the pudding in this way keeps it wonderfully moist, as the steam from the water stops the pudding from drying out. Serve with a spoonful of clotted cream and a pot of tea.

CHAPTER FOUR

PMT

For the times when only chocolate will do

Okay, okay – I admit it. Like most girls I don't really need much of an excuse to reach for the chocolate, but there are times in a woman's life when only its melting velvetiness will do. Besides, I've figured out that it's a pretty safe way of dealing with all the dramas life sometimes deals you. From a cheating boyfriend to hormonal mood swings, a chunk of chocolate is the only thing that will help the bitterness go down.

Chefs value hefty bars of 70% cocoa as though they were made of gold, and as much as I appreciate their indulgent pleasure and often beautiful wrapping (yes, dear reader – I have a packaging fetish), I too enjoy the grainy saturated fat a Mars bar will leave on the roof of your mouth.

Now, pick up your spoon and sate your cravings.

CHEEKY CHOCOLATINIS

Who says you shouldn't drink alone?

MAKES 2 CHOCOLATE-FUELLED COCKTAILS

crushed ice
125ml/4fl oz chocolate
   liqueur
100ml/3½fl oz vodka
30g/generous 1oz
   good-quality dark
   chocolate, grated
a few curls of orange
   zest

I quite like to sip a couple of these alone in moments of pre-menstrual stress – and, yes, they help! And now with the nicotine ban firmly in place, chocolate and booze is the new cigarettes and alcohol – it's far more social, even if you are having a cheeky lonesome one!

Fill a cocktail shaker with crushed ice and pour in the chocolate liqueur and vodka. Shake it like Tom Cruise has nothing on you, and then strain into two martini glasses or espresso cups. Sprinkle with the dark chocolate and garnish with orange zest. Clink and drink.

THE BEST-EVER HOT CHOCOLATE

Ditch the tasteless, lo-cal instant hot chocolate for something a little more sumptuous. This is the drink of the goddesses. You know you're worth it.

In a saucepan, heat the milk, cream, sugar, vanilla pod, cocoa, salt and orange zest until simmering. Simmer over a low heat for about 5 minutes, making sure it doesn't boil.

In a double boiler, melt the chocolate and then strain the milk over it. Discard the solids except for the vanilla pod (which you can dry and stick in some sugar to make vanilla sugar). Mix well and carry on heating until it is hot – and I mean hot; hot chocolate should never be lukewarm. Whisk it up until very frothy and then pour into cups and top each with a large marshmallow. Put up a 'Do not Disturb' sign and sip.

MAKES 2

200ml/7fl oz full-fat milk
35ml/1¼fl oz double cream
2 tsp brown sugar
1 vanilla pod, split lengthways
15g/½oz quality cocoa powder
1 pinch of sea salt
zest of ½ orange
50g/2oz very good-quality
   dark chocolate (at least
    70% cocoa solids)
2 marshmallows

KITCHEN-ADE

A double boiler, or bain-marie, simply consists of a saucepan with a heatproof bowl fitted on it. The pan underneath is partially filled with water brought to a boil, to give the bowl an indirect heat. The bottom of the bowl should not touch the water. It's a great method for cooking heat-sensitive ingredients such as chocolate and eggs, or delicate cream sauces that break down with direct heat.

Make your hot chocolate a little devilish by pouring in 2 tablespoons of brandy once it's ready.

DOUBLE-CHOCOLATE ORANGE BROWNIES

If you're a rampant chocoholic looking for your next hit, these rich, gooey brownies are guaranteed to leave you with a high.

SERVES 12 OR 1 – SURELY THAT'S UP TO YOU

225g/8oz unsalted butter, plus extra to grease
225g/8oz dark chocolate, roughly broken
4 eggs
300g/10oz golden caster sugar
2 tsp vanilla extract
zest of 1 orange
2 tbsp orange juice
½ tsp sea salt
150g/5oz plain flour
1 tsp baking powder
100g/3½oz white chocolate chips

Just one more bite? Well, there are worse things to be addicted to...

Preheat the oven to 180°C/350°F/gas 4. Grease and line a 20×20cm/8×8in baking sheet, or use a small roasting tin.

Put the butter and chocolate into a heatproof bowl over a pan of hot water and leave to melt. In a bowl, beat the eggs and then add the sugar, vanilla, orange zest and juice and salt. Next, fold in the flour and baking powder. Pour in the gloriously silky liquid chocolate, chuck in the chocolate chips and give it one last stir.

Pour the batter into the baking sheet or tin and bake for 35–40 minutes. Test it with a skewer – it should be thin and crisp on the top, and gooey but not raw in the middle. Leave it to cool before cutting it or removing from the tin.

WHITE CHOCOLATE AND BLUEBERRY CRUMBLE MUFFINS

These muffins are so packed with antioxidant blueberries that you needn't feel too guilty about having a little nibble.

MAKES ABOUT 16 FAT MUFFINS

For the muffin batter
450g/1lb plain flour
2½ tsp baking powder
175g/6oz golden caster sugar
½ tsp sea salt
zest of ½ lemon
200g/7oz white chocolate, chopped into chunks
250g/7oz blueberries
50ml/2fl oz melted unsalted butter
350ml/12fl oz full-fat milk
1 large egg, beaten

For the crumble
50g/2oz plain flour
65g/2½oz golden caster sugar
½ tsp ground cinnamon
25g/1oz unsalted butter

The chewy crumble topping makes these especially moreish, and I just love the way the berries burst and stain the muffin cases with their inky violet dye as they bake.

Preheat the oven to 190°C/375°F/gas 5. Line two muffin tins with muffin cases.

Begin by preparing the crumble mixture. In a bowl, mix the flour, sugar and cinnamon. Chop the butter into squares and then, using your fingers, rub it into the flour until the mixture forms a breadcrumb texture. Leave any lumps – these are going to add to the chewiness of your muffin.

Now, the main event. Sift the flour and baking powder into a bowl and then stir in the sugar and salt. Add the lemon zest, chocolate and blueberries, then pour in the butter, milk and egg and mix to bind. The mixing doesn't take any real effort here – just mix until the ingredients have all amalgamated.

Spoon the batter into the muffin cases more or less to the top. Scatter on the crumble topping and bake for about 25 minutes. Use a skewer to check if the cakes are ready – it should come out clean as a pin if they are.

These are best eaten cool, but I wouldn't blame you if you couldn't resist just one hot one.

MIDNIGHT MUNCHIES COOKIES

I'm a stickler for tidiness, but when it comes to my bed, you'll always find the odd crumb – I guess that's just the way the cookie crumbles.

MAKES 12 LARGE COOKIES

125g/4oz unsalted butter, softened
175g/6oz golden caster sugar
1 large egg
100g/3½oz dark chocolate chips
2 tsp vanilla extract
150g/5oz plain flour
½ tsp bicarbonate of soda
½ tsp sea salt

These giant chewy ones, along with a glass of milk, are the *only* cure for my insomnia.

Preheat the oven to 180°C/350°F/gas 4. Line a couple of large baking sheets with baking parchment.

Cream the butter and sugar together until light and fluffy, then beat in the egg, chocolate chips and vanilla extract. Sift in the flour, bicarbonate of soda and salt and mix well to combine all the ingredients.

Divide the mixture into twelve portions. Roll each one into a rough ball and then flatten slightly on the trays. Make sure they are well spaced out, as these do have a tendency to spread their wings when baking.

Bake for 12–15 minutes for delightfully chewy cookies. Let them cool and harden before you lift them from the baking sheet. Once they are cooler, lift them off the baking parchment and transfer them onto a wire cooling rack. Serve with a glass of chilled milk or a cup of tea.

GOOEY CHOCOLATE MALT PUDDINGS

These puddings are the halfway house between a sponge and a soufflé.

They're firm and springy on the outside, with a well of muddy chocolate sauce on the inside. Gilding the lily with this pud is near on impossible – but by all means embellish it with a scoop of vanilla ice cream or velvety single cream.

Preheat the oven to 180°C/350°F/gas 4. Lightly butter 8 ramekin dishes.

Whisk together the butter and caster sugar until light and fudgy. Add the eggs, one at a time, and beat in well to combine. Sift in the flour, baking powder, cocoa and malted milk powder and mix, then pour in the milk, a little at a time. Stir until beautifully smooth, then mix in the chocolate chips. Divide the mixture between the ramekins.

For the gooey middle, combine the soft brown sugar, malted milk powder and cocoa with the boiling water. Stir until it is well mixed, then pour over each pudding, dividing it equally amongst them. Bake for 20–25 minutes until the puddings are just set on the top and gooey in the middle.

SERVES 8

150g/5oz unsalted butter, softened, plus extra to grease
250g/9oz golden caster sugar
3 eggs
225g/8oz self-raising flour
1 tsp baking powder
50g/2oz good-quality cocoa powder
60g/2¼oz malted milk powder
250ml/8fl oz full-fat milk
150g/5oz dark chocolate chips

For the sauce
150g/5oz soft brown sugar
40g/1½oz malted milk powder
25g/1oz cocoa powder
350ml/12fl oz boiling water

BANANA & CHOCOLATE CHIP LOAF

If you're looking for a lighter-than-a-supermodel-at-fashion-week cake, then I suggest you turn the page now.

SERVES 8

250g/9oz plain flour
1 tsp baking powder
1 tsp bicarbonate of soda
1 pinch of sea salt
150g/5oz dark chocolate
   chips
100g/3½oz chopped walnuts
50g/2oz unsalted butter
225g/8oz caster sugar
2 large eggs
3 medium bananas, mashed
2 tsp vanilla extract

This cake is unashamedly dense with nuts, bitter chocolate and sweet mushy bananas. It's the heavyweight champion of cakes, and worth every chocoholic calorie you spend on it.

Preheat the oven to 180°C/350°F/gas 4. Line a large loaf tin with greaseproof paper.

Mix the flour, baking powder, bicarbonate of soda and salt in a bowl. In another bowl, mix the chocolate chips with the walnuts and coat well with 1 tablespoon of the flour mixture.

In a mixing bowl or food processor, cream the butter and then add the sugar. Beat in the eggs, one at a time, and then pour in the mashed bananas and vanilla extract. You should now have a lovely, loose yellow batter. Finally, fold in the flour mixture and beat until you have a thick cake batter.

Pour one-third of the batter into the loaf tin, sprinkle with half the chocolate and walnut mixture and top with another third of the batter. Layer again with the remaining chocolate and walnut mix, then cover with the remaining batter. Run a knife through the depth of the batter in a zigzag pattern to disperse the chocolate and nuts.

Bake in the oven for 1 hour. Test it with a skewer to check it is cooked – if not, bake for a further 15 minutes. Let it cool completely before attempting to turn it out. Slice into thick slabs once cool.

FROZEN CHOCOLATE BANANAS

Here's an easy way to go from a squishy sad banana to top banana.

Line a baking sheet with baking parchment. Insert a lolly stick or a small wooden skewer in each banana half so it looks like a lolly. Lay them on the baking sheet and freeze for 20 minutes to harden.

Put the chocolate into a heatproof bowl along with the vegetable oil and melt over a pan of boiling water. Stir until it's molten and glossy.

Roll each banana half in the chocolate and then top with the nuts. Freeze again until the chocolate sets.

MAKES 8

4 bananas, peeled and halved
170g/scant 6oz dark chocolate, roughly chopped
2 tbsp vegetable oil
100g/3½oz chopped nuts

KITCHEN-ADE

To make these for children, replace the dark chocolate with milk chocolate and the nuts with 60g/2¼oz of hundreds and thousands sprinkles.

RASPBERRY & BITTER CHOCOLATE LOLLIES

These popsicles are decadently delicious – the tart raspberries and bitter chocolate are a luxurious combination.

If you're cooking for grown ups, I urge you to add a splash of crème de framboise, or even a little vodka will do. Virgin or not – these are the perfect pudding on a stick.

Place the raspberries, sugar, lemon juice and water in a pan and slowly bring it up to the boil. Remove from the heat and leave to cool.

Pour in the raspberry liqueur, if you're using it, at this stage. Push the mixture through a fine mesh sieve set over a bowl and discard the seeds.

Divide the mixture between 8 lolly moulds – I fill them up three-quarters of the way in – and then freeze until partially frozen. This should take just 30 minutes.

Meanwhile, get on with making the chocolate ice. Bring the double cream to simmer in a saucepan and then remove from the heat. Stir the chocolate in until it's a silky melt.

Remove the raspberry ices from the freezer and top up the moulds with the chocolate. Return to the freezer until set.

KITCHEN-ADE
To remove the ice lollies from their moulds, dip the bottom of the moulds in a dish of warm water – this should loosen them up and help them slide out easily.

MAKES 8 LUSCIOUS LOLLIES

For the raspberry ice
300g/10oz frozen or fresh raspberries
50g/2oz caster sugar
juice of 1 lemon
450ml/15fl oz cold water
2 tbsp raspberry liqueur (optional)

For the chocolate ice layer
200ml/7fl oz double cream
100g/3½oz dark chocolate, roughly chopped

TURKISH DELIGHT FRUIT & NUT ROCKY ROAD

This is a treasure trove of a refrigerator cake studded with nuts, raisins, biscuit and, of course, jewels of swoon-some Turkish Delight. This makes a great gift, should you decide to share it.

SERVES 12

200g/7oz dark chocolate, roughly chopped
125ml/4fl oz double cream
125g/4oz digestive biscuits
40g/1½oz pistachios, halved
40g/1½oz toasted flaked almonds
40g/½oz raisins
3 × 55g Fry's Turkish Delight, chopped into cubes

Line an 18×18cm/7×7in baking tin with cling film, leaving enough hanging over the rim to wrap up the cake entirely.

In a double boiler, melt the chocolate, then whisk in the cream until you have a silky molten chocolate sauce. Set it aside to cool slightly.

Meanwhile, in a mixing bowl, coarsely crush the digestives with the end of a rolling pin and combine with the pistachios, almonds, raisins and Turkish Delight. Pour the cooled chocolate into the bowl and stir to coat all the fruit, nuts and biscuit rubble.

Turn the sticky mix out into the tin, pressing it down firmly. Refrigerate to set for 4–6 hours. Slice into squares when it has set.

CHOCOLATE ICE-CREAM PIE

This cake is rapturously good, yet it requires no hard labour – just a little bit of bashing and mixing.

What's more, you can keep it in the freezer for at least a week, so you have instant chocoholic gratification on demand.

Preheat the oven to 170°C/325°F/gas 3. Put the custard creams into a plastic freezer bag and bash with a rolling pin until you are left with biscuity gravel. Empty out into a bowl, pour the melted butter into the bowl and mix well. Press the mixture over the base of a 20cm/8in springform cake tin and bake for 15 minutes. Set it aside to cool.

Mix the ice cream with the bashed up Maltesers and then smooth the mixture over the cooled biscuit base. Dot the walnut halves evenly around the edge and freeze until set.

Cut into thick slices and serve with a little warm chocolate sauce.

SERVES 8–10

200g/7oz custard creams
60g/2¼oz unsalted butter, melted
1 litre/1¾ pints chocolate ice cream
150g/5oz Maltesers, bashed into a coarse rubble
12 walnut halves
a drizzle of good-quality chocolate sauce

V. remote
control and a
meal for one

We all need a little me-time

Reasons to appreciate a night in on your own:

1 You have the remote control to yourself.
2 You can walk around in the tattiest but most comfy pair of trackies –
   no dressing for dinner required.
3 Caring doesn't have to be sharing – you can eat a meal for one without having to offer up the last potato.

Finding yourself alone on a Friday night should be a celebration, not a
time to drown yourself in a chips, dips and Häagen-Dazs dinner for one.
You'll only be remorseful the morning after! Meals for one don't have to
be fussy or hard work. I like to use my me-time to pack in a face pack,
manicure and pedicure.

Here are some of my favourite lonesome eats – the perfect size for a party
of one.

POLLACK WITH CHORIZO, CANNELLINI BEANS & SWISS CHARD

This recipe is inspired by the Spanish tradition of combining white fish with meaty, paprika sausage.

I love the way the chorizo oozes its rich hot oil into the broth and tinges the pale fish and beans with its sunset stain. This makes a really hearty Friday-night supper for one.

Heat the olive oil in a pan and fry the chorizo until crisp and its crimson tarnish has seeped into the oil. Add the garlic and fry until fragrant, then tumble in the cannellini beans. Stir until the beans are well coated with the paprika oil, then pour in the wine along with the saffron. Boil the wine rapidly until it has reduced by half.

Season the fish on both sides with salt and pepper. Put the chard into the cannellini bean and chorizo broth and then lay the fish over it. Cover the pan, lower the heat and let the fish steam for 6 minutes or until it is opaque.

Sprinkle with the lemon juice and serve with a wedge of lemon and some bread to soak up the hearty broth.

SERVES 1

a glug of olive oil
50g/2oz uncooked chorizo
   sausage, sliced
1 garlic clove, chopped
100g/3½oz tinned cannellini
   beans, drained and rinsed
125ml/4fl oz white wine
1 pinch of saffron strands
   pounded in a little
   warm water
1 fillet of pollack, about
   150g/5oz
sea salt and freshly ground
   black pepper
1 handful of Swiss chard,
   chopped
juice of ½ lemon
lemon wedge, to serve

CHILLI CHEESE TOASTS

Sometimes the very pleasure of eating alone is enjoying simple, humble food.

SERVES 1

½ small red onion, finely
  chopped
1 tomato, finely chopped
1 green chilli (deseeded if
  you don't want it too
  spicy), finely chopped
¼ green pepper, deseeded
  and finely chopped
3 tbsp chopped fresh
  coriander
2 tsp sweet chilli sauce or
  tomato ketchup
freshly ground black pepper
2 slices of thick white bread
100g/3½oz Cheddar cheese,
  grated

I could quite easily hoover up a hulk of cheese with a thin white baguette or some crackers, but I also love the informality of these easy chilli cheese toasts. Like pizza, they don't need a fork and knife, so you can eat while watching trashy TV or reading – in fact, you can do all three at once if you so please: the ultimate tasty multi-tasking with no interruptions.

Preheat the grill. Mix together the onion, tomato, chilli, green pepper, coriander and sweet chilli sauce or tomato ketchup. Season with pepper.

Toast one side of the bread under the grill, then layer the vegetable mix over the untoasted side of the bread. Flash under the grill for 3 minutes, so the onion softens slightly, then top with the cheese and cook until golden and bubbling. Serve immediately with a generous helping of trash TV.

PEA, PANCETTA & HALLOUMI FRITTATA

When you want something that goes from stove to plate in a matter of minutes, you can always rely on eggs.

This Italian omelette is truly fuss-free and uses ingredients such as the under-rated frozen pea, which you are likely to have in stock. It really is a stress-free after-work supper. Use a non-stick pan to avoid any disappointing disasters when inverting the omelette onto a plate.

Preheat the grill. Heat the olive oil in a frying pan over a low heat and then gently sauté the onion and garlic until soft. Add the pancetta or bacon and fry until golden brown and crisp. Stir in the peas and parsley.

In a bowl, beat the eggs with the cream and seasoning. Pour the egg into the frying pan and gently flick back the edges with a knife, so the runny egg seeps over and begins to set. After 3 minutes, place the halloumi over the surface of the egg and put the pan under the grill.

Remove from the grill once it is just set and the halloumi is a little toasted. Serve with some dressed rocket and an unwinding glass of wine.

SERVES 1

1 tsp olive oil
½ small red onion, sliced
1 garlic clove, chopped
40g/1½oz pancetta or rindless
    streaky bacon, cubed
1 handful of frozen peas
1 tbsp chopped fresh
    flat-leaf parsley
3 eggs
3 tbsp double cream
sea salt and freshly ground
    black pepper
4 slices of halloumi cheese
rocket dressed with a little
    vinaigrette, to serve

KITCHEN-ADE
If you don't have halloumi, goat's cheese and feta work equally well.

ROSEMARY & CHILLI-SEARED
TUNA WITH CARAMELISED LEMONY ARTICHOKES

As much as I enjoy the theatre of entertaining, I am also drawn to the narcissistic indulgence of cooking for just me.

On occasion I pamper myself: I use the best ingredients I can lay my hands on and serve it up on my best china – well, everyone has an ego to feed, after all!

Cooking for yourself also leaves room to experiment – it's only yourself you have to impress and if it all goes horribly wrong you can always dial out for a pizza. This just-sealed tuna, crusty on the outside and still juicily pink on the inside, with some perky artichokes, was one of my experimental successes – it beats a take-out any time.

In a pestle and mortar, pound the garlic, rosemary, lemon zest and chilli flakes together with salt and pepper to taste. Pour in the lemon juice and olive oil and mix well. Anoint the tuna with the seasoned oil, making sure it is coated on both sides. Leave it to marinate at room temperature for 20 minutes.

Heat a griddle pan until very hot, then sear the tuna for 2 minutes on each side. It should still be pink in the middle. Transfer to a warm plate and leave to rest.

Meanwhile, slice the artichokes in half if they are still whole and place them on the griddle, cut-side down. Leave them on the pan for a minute until they are charred, then turn them over, sprinkle with sugar and give them a squeeze of lemon juice. Move them around in the pan until they are slightly caramelised and serve up with the warm tuna.

SERVES 1

1 garlic clove
1 tsp rosemary leaves, finely chopped
1 tsp lemon zest
½ tsp chilli flakes
sea salt and freshly ground black pepper
1 tbsp lemon juice
2 tbsp olive oil
1 tuna steak

For the caramelised lemony artichokes

50g/2oz tinned artichoke hearts in olive oil, drained
1 tsp caster sugar
lemon juice

SOFT-BOILED EGGS WITH ASPARAGUS

The pleasure of cooking for one is sometimes obscured by complicated recipes.

SERVES 1

2 large eggs
8 spears of asparagus, the
    woody stems snapped off
a few drops of Tabasco
sea salt and freshly ground
    black pepper

Keeping it simple doesn't mean you have to compromise on taste – this light supper is one of my favourites and means you'll be out of the kitchen in less than 10 minutes.

Simmer the eggs in boiling water for 5 minutes. Meanwhile, steam the asparagus for 5 minutes – it should still be snappish and sprightly. Crack the tops off the eggs and season with Tabasco, salt and pepper. Serve with the asparagus dippers. Blissful eating in less than 10 minutes.

THAI COCONUT CHICKEN SOUP

If soups could purge gastronomic sins, this would be the one that did it.

I am not talking in riddles here – this soup's got a wonderfully healing quality. Try it and your stomach will know exactly what I mean!

If I am honest, I never have the time to make stock from scratch. I always forget to reserve the chicken carcass or never plan that far ahead, so it's a small mercy that there are so many good ready-made chicken stocks available to buy now.

In a saucepan, bring the chicken stock to the boil, then add the ginger, galangal (if you're using it), lime zest, lemon grass and chillies. Cover and simmer for about 10 minutes.

Stir in the chicken, coconut milk, sugar and fish sauce and simmer again until the chicken is cooked and tender – about 12 minutes. Finally, pour in the lime juice and add plenty of fresh coriander. Serve steaming.

MAKES ENOUGH FOR 2 GREEDY HELPINGS OR 4 MODEST ONES

300ml/10fl oz chicken stock

3cm/1¼in piece of fresh root ginger, peeled and cut into thin strips

2 tsp grated galangal (optional)

zest of 1 lime

1 lemon grass stick, finely chopped

2 red chillies (deseeded if you don't want it too spicy), thinly sliced

250g/9oz skinned, boned chicken thighs, cut into 1cm/1½in chunks

300ml/10fl oz coconut milk

2 tbsp caster sugar

4 tbsp nam pla (fish sauce)

juice of 2 limes

6 heaped tbsp chopped fresh coriander

POT-ROAST CHICKEN

WITH PRESERVED LEMONS & HERBY COUSCOUS

This is my take on a Moroccan tagine – it takes no time at all to prepare and there's barely a dish to wash up afterwards.

When a plate of food is packed with as many friendly flavours as this one is, you won't even miss having company.

Gently heat some olive oil in a casserole dish, then add the onion and cook until it's translucent and caught at the edges. Add the chicken thighs (you can use breast, but thighs are so much juicier and not to mention cheaper!) and fry until golden all over, then throw in the turmeric, ginger and garlic. Fry briefly again until fragrant, then add the preserved lemons and olives, stir and pour in the chicken stock. Bring to the boil, then cover and simmer on a low heat for about 12 minutes, by which time the chicken should be tender and cooked through. Take the pan off the heat, fish the chicken out of the liquid and set aside.

Pour the couscous into the liquid, cover the pan and leave for 5 minutes. After 5 minutes are up, uncover, scatter in the herbs and fluff up with a fork. Drizzle with some extra virgin olive oil, return the chicken to the pan and serve. You may not even want to wait to get it onto a plate!

SERVES 1

3 tbsp olive oil
1 small red onion, finely sliced
2 chicken thighs, skin and bone on/in
¼ tsp turmeric
½ tsp freshly grated root ginger
1 garlic clove, chopped
2–3 large or 6 small preserved lemons (see page 55), chopped
6 large green olives
200ml/7fl oz chicken stock
75g/3oz couscous
2 tbsp each of chopped fresh coriander, mint and flat-leaf parsley
extra virgin olive oil, to drizzle

MAPLE MUSTARD PORK CHOP
WITH CHILLI, LEMON & GARLIC-FRIED CURLY KALE

Get your chops around my ultimate Monday evening supper – just the thing to look forward to after a manic day at work.

Start it off on Sunday evening by marinating the meat – the marinade will take no more than 10 minutes to whip up – and all you'll have to do when you walk through the door ravenous is grill or fry the pork for 5 minutes on each side. The maple syrup together with the sweet, golden rind of fat on the pork pair exceptionally well with a bed of robust, garlicky kale.

Cut off the excess fat from the pork chop, but don't get carried away or you'll end up with meat that's as tough as old boots. Lay the chop in a dish and scatter on the lemon zest, thyme, garlic and salt to taste. Whisk the maple syrup, lemon juice, light soy sauce, grain mustard and olive oil together and pour over the chop. Cover with cling film and marinate for a few hours or overnight.

Heat a pan or a grill until sizzling. Scrape the excess marinade off the meat and reserve it for basting. Cook the chop for 5 minutes on each side, basting with the marinade as you cook. Put the chop on a warm plate and leave to rest while you cook the kale.

Wipe the excess marinade from the pan. Warm the olive oil, add the garlic and chilli flakes and fry until pale golden. Add the kale and stir-fry for 4 minutes. Drizzle with the lemon juice and serve piled high next to the chop.

KITCHEN-ADE
If you want your chop to cook super fast, lay cling film over it and bash it with a mallet, so that it is thin and flat. This guarantees even cooking and, after a stressful day, a bit of mallet action is quite therapeutic.

SERVES 1

1 boneless pork chop
1 tsp lemon zest
leaves stripped from
   1 sprig of thyme
1 garlic clove, sliced
sea salt
3 tsp maple syrup
1 tbsp lemon juice
1 tbsp olive oil
2 tsp light soy sauce
2 tsp grain mustard

For the curly kale
a drizzle of olive oil
1 garlic clove, crushed
1 pinch of chilli flakes
100g/3½oz curly kale
2 tbsp lemon juice

THAI CURRY MUSSELS

Cooking for one shouldn't just mean popping a meal in a microwave and scoffing it before you've even sat down.

It should be an opportunity to bask in the comfort of your own company – a celebration of yourself, if you like. These mussels in a fragrant Thai broth are extravagant, but simple to do, thanks to the convenience of a ready-made curry paste. If you can spoil friends and lovers, why shouldn't you make a fuss of number one?

Heat the vegetable oil in a saucepan. Add the tomato, garlic and ginger and sauté until the ginger and garlic are aromatic. Stir in the coconut milk, curry paste and half the coriander and simmer for 3–4 minutes to blend the flavours.

Add the mussels, cover and cook until they open – this should take just 5 minutes. Discard any mussels that do not open. Season the broth with the fish sauce and simmer again for 1 minute. Finally, pour in the lime juice and strew with the remaining coriander. Eat as they are or with some steamed rice.

SERVES 1

1 tbsp vegetable oil
1 large tomato, chopped
1 garlic clove, crushed
1 tsp freshly grated root ginger
200ml/7fl oz coconut milk
1 tsp Thai red curry paste
4 tbsp chopped fresh
   coriander
500g/1lb 2oz mussels,
   scrubbed and debearded
1 tbsp nam pla (fish sauce)
1 tbsp lime juice

CHAPTER SIX

Social grazing

Lots of Martinis and food to pick at

I recently overheard a stylish journalist saying that her diet consisted of cigarettes, champagne and canapés. She'd had beluga blinis, sushi supplied by Nobu, and moreish little macaroons that would have made Marie Antoinette salivate. I winced at the thought of anyone offering her cheese and pineapple on a stick – eeek!

Though I am quite happy to be offered a pig in a blanket and a glass of chilled Chablis, I know that there's more to putting on a party spread for your best friends than a trip to the chilled section of your local supermarket.

I'm not asking you to turn all Stepford wives and bake bread without splitting a glossy blow-dried hair – party food can be low effort and high on taste. Try these easy-peasy party pleasers and make your parties the hottest ticket in town!

HUMMUS

Dips that you can scoop up on pitta bread are a sure-fire hit at a party.

SERVES 4–6

300g/10oz tinned chickpeas,
    drained and rinsed
1 fat garlic clove, roughly
    chopped
2 tbsp tahini (see Kitchen-ade)
2 tbsp lemon juice
2 tbsp natural yoghurt
sea salt

To serve

1 tbsp chopped fresh flat-leaf
    parsley
1 pinch of cayenne pepper
1 tbsp olive oil, to drizzle

I like to lay out huge bowls of them, sprinkled with parsley and dotted with the odd olive or two. You can buy good shop-bought hummus these days, but when knocking up a tastier, fresher version at home is just a matter of pressing a button on a food processor, why bother? Peas out!

Put the chickpeas, garlic, tahini, lemon juice, yoghurt and salt to taste into a food processor and whiz to a smooth paste. Pour into a serving dish and then scatter with the parsley, cayenne pepper and a drizzle of olive oil.

You can also garnish the hummus with a whole host of other toppings, including chilli flakes, toasted pine nuts, olives, hard-boiled eggs, or sliced gherkins.

KITCHEN-ADE

Tahini is a Middle Eastern paste made from crushed sesame seeds. It's gluey and murky, but transforms once it's poured into sauces and dressings. It gives hummus a wonderfully earthy flavour and silky texture. Look out for it in Middle Eastern food stores.

For a spruced-up red pepper hummus, simply add 1 roasted red pepper to the mix.

BABA GANOUSH

This silky mush of garlic-pungent smoky aubergine paste is truly satisfying.

Eat it shovelled onto puffs of hot Middle Eastern bread for best effect, or serve it as a side dish to a whole roasted leg of lamb.

Preheat the grill to hot. Pierce the aubergines several times with a fork, place them under the grill and cook until soft. Keep turning the aubergines over so they are evenly cooked throughout. This should take 15–20 minutes. Once they're cooked, leave them to cool.

Peel the aubergines and discard the skins – they should come off very easily. Roughly chop the flesh and blend it with the remaining ingredients in a food processor until you have a sleek paste.

Sprinkle with the paprika and chopped parsley and serve with warm shards of pitta bread.

SERVES 6

2 large aubergines
50g/2oz natural yoghurt
50ml/2fl oz tahini
 (see page 132)
juice of 1 lemon
1 garlic clove, crushed
2 tsp ground cumin
5 heaped tbsp chopped fresh
 coriander

To garnish and serve
1 tsp hot paprika
1 tbsp chopped fresh flat-leaf
 parsley
pitta bread

SQUID WITH POTATOES & PAPRIKA

I first ate a version of this dish when I was on holiday in
Zaragossa.

SERVES 4–6

500g/1lb 2oz baby squid

2–3 large waxy potatoes,
    such as La Ratte, cut
    into chunky wedges

7 tbsp olive oil

25g/1oz unsalted butter

2 bay leaves

½ head of garlic, unpeeled

sea salt and freshly ground
    black pepper

juice of 1 lemon

2 heaped tsp good-quality
    Spanish paprika, plus
    extra to sprinkle

1 tablespoon chopped fresh
    flat-leaf parsley

extra virgin olive oil, to
    drizzle

The backstreet tapas bar that served it up seemed to get
through piles and piles of it. There is something about being
able to pick at it with your fingers that makes it very sociable
eating. It was so delicious, in fact, that I went back for second
helpings the very next day – only to find, disappointingly, the
restaurant shut! I had no other option but to try and recreate
it when I got back home. The garlicky paprika-infused oil
will leave you licking your fingers.

Clean and prepare the squid – this is easy once you know
how. Pull out the tentacles from the main tube. The insides
should also fall out quite easily. Cut the tentacles off just
underneath the squid's eyes and reserve – these are edible.
Pull out and discard the long plastic-like spine from inside
the body of the squid, then scrape the dark outer membrane
off the flesh with the back of a knife until you're left with the
pure white flesh and tentacles. Slit the squid on one side and
open it out. Score it diagonally on the inside in two directions
to make a diamond pattern, or just cut it into rings.

Bring a large pan of water to the boil and throw in
plenty of salt. Add the potatoes and boil for about 6 minutes
until the edges are slightly broken down, then drain. Heat
5 tablespoons of olive oil with the butter in a large frying pan
– you want to cook the potatoes in a single layer. Throw in
the bay leaves and garlic (no need to peel it – it's just there
to add a subtle background flavour) and, once sizzling,
add the potatoes in a single layer. Turn down the heat to
medium and cook, turning to catch them on all sides,
until the potatoes crisp up and are a deep golden brown.

When the potatoes are almost ready, heat a griddle pan until very hot, brush your squid with the remaining olive oil and season with salt and pepper. Once the griddle is piping hot, grill the squid for 1 minute on each side until charred but still tender.

Using a slotted spoon, fish out the potatoes from their garlicky oil and arrange on a plate. Place the squid on top. Squeeze the lemon juice into the oil in the pan and stir in the paprika. Strain it, then pour the lemony oil over the squid and potatoes and finish with some chopped fresh parsley, a drizzle of extra virgin olive oil and a final sprinkling of paprika. Warning – this is addictive eating.

KITCHEN-ADE
The fresher your squid, the more tender it will be. Squid is fresh when it smells like the sea, not fishy or strong. It should be firm and glossy, not dull and sagging.

FALAFEL

These are one of THE best things to come out of chickpeas.

MAKES ABOUT 30

200g/7oz dried chickpeas,
    soaked in water overnight
    and drained
1 green chilli (deseeded if
    you don't want it too
    spicy), finely chopped
4 heaped tbsp roughly
    chopped fresh coriander
4 heaped tbsp roughly
    chopped fresh flat-leaf
    parsley
50g/2oz bulgur wheat
1 medium onion, very finely
    chopped
4 garlic cloves, crushed
2 tsp baking powder
2 tbsp tahini (see page 132)
juice of 1 lemon
2 tsp cumin seeds
2 tsp coriander seeds
sea salt
vegetable oil for deep-frying
    (see Cook's Notes, page 12)

I love their super-crisp shells, their garlicky, spice-laden flavour and the way they ooze a little in the middle when they are fresh out of the frying pan. Even the most bloodthirsty carnivore won't miss meat when chomping on these. For the ultimate sandwich, try them wrapped in pillowy hot pitta bread with pickled cucumbers, chilli sauce and shredded cabbage.

Place the chickpeas, chilli, coriander and parsley in a food processor and blitz until you have a breadcrumb-like texture. Tip out into a mixing bowl and add the bulgur wheat, onion, garlic, baking powder, tahini and lemon juice.

Dry-roast the cumin and coriander seeds in a hot pan – as soon as they become aromatic, take them off the heat and crush into a coarse powder. Mix the spices into the falafel mixture and stir well. Cover with cling film and chill in the fridge for 30 minutes. Add salt to taste only when you are absolutely ready to cook, as it draws out water from the onion and will turn your firm mixture into a sodden mess.

Heat the vegetable oil in a deep-fat fryer until it's shimmering and hot and then lower the heat to medium. While it's heating, take heaped tablespoons of the mixture, roll them into tight balls and flatten slightly. Deep-fry in batches for 3–4 minutes or until they're nutty brown. Drain well on kitchen paper. These are delicious hot or cold, with flat bread or just as they are.

BATATA HARA

The Spanish have patatas bravas, but I adore this Lebanese version full of assorted vegetables and dressed up in a spicy sauce.

If you don't want to fry the vegetables, roast them instead with a little olive oil until they're charred and golden and then dress them with the sauce – a welcome alternative to traditional roasted vegetables.

Heat the groundnut oil in a deep-fat fryer and fry all the vegetables until tender and golden brown, then drain.

To make the dressing, whisk the lemon juice, ketchup, spices and seasoning in a bowl. Pour over the vegetables and toss together until they are thoroughly coated. Top with the chopped coriander and eat immediately.

SERVES 6

groundnut oil for deep-frying (see Cook's Notes, page 12)
1 large waxy potato, such as Desiree, diced into medium cubes
1 orange-fleshed sweet potato, diced into medium cubes
1 small courgette, trimmed and sliced into chunks
8 cauliflower florets, halved
1 red pepper, deseeded and cut into large chunks
1 generous handful of chopped fresh coriander leaves, to serve

For the dressing
juice of 1 lemon
1 tbsp tomato ketchup
3 garlic cloves, crushed
1 heaped tsp ground coriander
½ tsp chilli powder
½ tsp hot paprika
¼ tsp ground mixed spice
sea salt and freshly ground black pepper

TABBOULEH

It's the perfect crunchy, refreshing salad for a hot summer barbecue.

100g/3½oz bulgur wheat
1 bunch of flat-leaf parsley, chopped
1 bunch of spring onions, finely chopped
4 ripe tomatoes, finely diced
1 Lebanese cucumber, finely diced
½ bunch of fresh mint, chopped
juice of 2 large juicy lemons
1 tsp toasted ground cumin
60ml/generous 2fl oz olive oil
1 tsp sea salt
freshly ground black pepper
crisp lettuce leaves, to serve

This is a knockout salad. Full of flat-leaf parsley, onion, tomato, cracked wheat and lemon juice, it packs a spirited punch. Eat it on its own to fully appreciate its mouth-puckering sharpness, or with some grilled chicken or bread to temper the tang.

Put the bulgur wheat into a bowl and cover with plenty of cold water. Cover the bowl and leave for about 20 minutes to soften. Drain it in a sieve and squeeze out as much excess water as possible.

Put the wheat into a salad bowl and then mix in the parsley, spring onions, tomatoes, cucumber, mint, lemon juice and cumin. Pour in the olive oil, add the salt and pepper to taste and give it all a hefty final mix. Serve piled up in a bowl with a few crisp lettuce leaves.

CHICKEN SKEWERS WITH GARLIC SAUCE

I adore nibbling on these chunks of chicken, enriched by a spicy marinade of lemon, garlic and olive oil.

SERVES 6

2 tbsp tomato ketchup
5 tbsp olive oil
4 garlic cloves, chopped
1 tsp cayenne pepper
1 tsp ground allspice
juice of 1 lemon
sea salt
700g/1½lb skinned, boned
    chicken thighs, cut into
    large cubes

For the garlic sauce
3 garlic cloves
½ tsp sea salt
juice of ½ lemon
1 egg yolk
150ml/5fl oz extra virgin
    olive oil

Personally, I like using thighs, as they tend to be juicier, but if you're fussy about bones, use chicken breast instead. Just make sure you keep basting the meat to stop it drying out. If you love garlic the way I do, you'll love the accompanying sauce – it'll have you hooked to your last lick.

Combine the ketchup, olive oil, chopped garlic, cayenne pepper, allspice, lemon juice and salt to taste to make a marinade. Place the chicken cubes in a large mixing bowl and pour the marinade over them. Mix well, then leave in the fridge to steep for at least 2 hours or overnight. Soak wooden skewers in water at the same time to stop them burning.

To make the garlic sauce, pound the garlic and salt together in a pestle and mortar until you have a thick paste. Transfer to a large bowl and add the lemon juice and egg yolk, then beat with an electric whisk until frothy. Pour in a steady trickle of extra virgin olive oil, whisking constantly until you have a light but thick sauce with the consistency of mayonnaise.

To cook the chicken, preheat the grill to its highest setting. Thread the chicken onto the skewers, place under the grill and cook for 5 minutes on each side or until the chicken is cooked through. Serve with a bowl of garlic sauce for dunking.

THAI FISHCAKES WITH FENNEL

Unlike English fishcakes, which are dense enough to use as shot-puts, these potato-less ones are delicate and dinky, making them the perfect party canapé.

In this recipe, the fennel adds an extra dimension of aniseedy flavour to an already spice-laden mix.

Chop all the fish into bite-sized chunks and put them into a food processor along with the coriander, lime zest, sugar and salt to taste. Whiz to a coarse paste. Empty into a mixing bowl and stir in the curry paste and fennel.

With oiled hands, take 2 tablespoons of the mixture in the palm of your hand, roll into a ball and then flatten into a patty. Repeat until you have about 30 little cakes.

Heat the groundnut oil in a deep-fat fryer and fry the fishcakes until they are golden brown. Serve with wedges of lime.

MAKES 30

300g/10oz skinless salmon fillets, pinboned
300g/10oz skinless white-fleshed fish fillets, such as pollack or cod, pinboned
3 tbsp chopped fresh coriander
grated zest of 1 lime
1 tbsp caster sugar
sea salt
4 heaped tbsp red curry paste
1 small fennel bulb, finely chopped
oil for greasing
groundnut oil for deep-frying (see Cook's Notes, page 12)
lime wedges, to serve

CRISPY SALT & PEPPER SQUID

This is one of the most popular starters at Chinese restaurants, so it's likely to go down a storm at a party.

It's remarkably easy to do, and you'll end up with the lightest squid that's as tender as the night.

Cut the squid into 2cm/¾in rings and pat dry with kitchen paper. Drying it like this will ensure extra crispiness.

Heat a dry frying pan and then toast all the peppercorns until they are aromatic. Put them into a pestle and mortar along with the salt and crush to a coarse powder. Empty into a bowl and mix with the cornflour.

Heat the groundnut oil in a deep-fat fryer over a high flame until shimmering. Place the squid in a bowl with the salt and pepper flour and mix well. Shake off the excess flour, then fry in the hot oil for 1 minute – fry for longer and you'll end up with squid that has the texture of a rubber band. Drain well on kitchen paper.

When you have finished frying the squid, remove most of the oil from the pan, bar a few tablespoons, and flash-fry the chillies, spring onions and garlic for 1 minute. Drain and mix well with the squid. Drizzle with the lime juice and sprinkle with the coriander. Don't waste any time in tucking in.

SERVES 8

1kg/2¼lb baby squid, cleaned and prepared (see page 134)
2 tsp black peppercorns
2 tsp Sichuan peppercorns
2 tsp sea salt
60g/2¼oz cornflour
groundnut oil for deep-frying (see Cook's Notes, page 12)
2 red chillies (deseeded if you don't want it too spicy), sliced
6 spring onions, sliced
4 garlic cloves, chopped
juice of ½ lime
4 heaped tbsp chopped fresh coriander

NO-COOK PRAWN & NOODLE SPRING ROLLS
WITH EASY CHILLI & PEANUT SAUCE

These, in effect, are beautiful parcels of herby Asian salad.

MAKES 32

125g/4oz cooked rice noodles

5 spring onions, cut into
fine strips

½ red pepper, deseeded and
cut into extra fine strips

50g/2oz beansprouts

2 tbsp finely chopped
fresh mint

2 tsp caster sugar

3 garlic cloves, crushed

juice of 1 lime

2 tsp rice vinegar

1 tbsp nam pla (fish sauce)

16 rice paper spring roll
wrappers (see Kitchen-ade)

32 cooked king prawns,
butterflied

16 small sprigs of coriander

**For the peanut and
sweet chilli dip**

60ml/generous 2fl oz
sweet chilli sauce

juice of 1 lime

4 tbsp crushed salted
peanuts

Don't be intimidated by them – they look terribly fiddly but aren't at all. Once you've got the conveyor belt of dipping, stuffing and rolling going, they are mindlessly relaxing to make. They're light and refreshing and are bound to wow your guests – just don't let on how simple they are!

To make the dip, combine all the ingredients in a bowl and stir well.

In a bowl, combine the cooked rice noodles, spring onions, red pepper, beansprouts, mint, sugar, garlic, lime juice, rice vinegar and fish sauce and mix well.

Dip the wrappers into hot water for 15 seconds, place on a tea towel and dab with another towel to remove excess water. Put 2 prawns vertically down the centre of one wrapper, leaving a 2cm/¾in space above and below the prawns. Next, top with a coriander sprig followed by a tablespoon or so of the noodle salad. Fold the bottom of the wrapper up over the filling. Fold in one side, then roll up tightly like a fat cigar. Repeat with the remaining ingredients to make 16 rolls. Cut the rolls diagonally in half through the middle and serve with the dipping sauce.

KITCHEN-ADE

Rice paper spring roll wrappers are readily available in most supermarkets, but if you can't get hold of them there they are widely available in Asian food stores.

You can also make these wraps using large lettuce leaves instead of the rice paper wrappers.

SPICY PRAWN BIG DIPPERS WITH CHILLI, LIME & ONION SALT

These sticky, spicy, more-ish prawn skewers are as lively as a fairground, packing in a rollercoaster of sweet, hot and sour sensations all at once.

MAKES 10 SKEWERS

25ml/1fl oz olive oil
juice of 1 lime
2 tbsp nam pla (fish sauce)
1 tbsp jaggery or soft brown
    sugar
1 red chilli (deseeded if you
    don't want it too spicy),
    finely chopped
5cm/2in knob of fresh root
    ginger, peeled and grated
3 garlic cloves, minced
40 raw tiger prawns, peeled
    and deveined

For the chilli, lime and onion salt

2 tsp dried chilli flakes
1 tbsp sea salt
2 tbsp caster sugar
finely grated zest of 1 lime
4 tbsp fried onions

Rather than serving them with a more traditional dipping sauce, I make up this punchy chilli salt. One dunk and you'll understand why I call them big dippers.

Whisk together the olive oil, lime juice and fish sauce and then add the jaggery or sugar, the red chilli, ginger and garlic. Add the prawns and stir well. Cover with cling film and leave to marinate for 30 minutes. Soak 10 wooden skewers in water at the same time.

Meanwhile, make the onion salt by pounding together all the ingredients in a pestle and mortar until you have a coarse powder.

To cook the prawns, heat a griddle pan until very hot. Thread 4 prawns onto each skewer and cook for 3 minutes on each side or until the prawns are pink and opaque. Dredge in the chilli, lime and onion salt and eat.

THAI AUBERGINE SALAD

Thailand is famous for its prickly spicy beef salad and this is my veggie-friendly take on it.

2 large aubergines, trimmed and sliced into thin rounds

olive oil for brushing

1 bunch each of fresh coriander and mint, roughly chopped

6 tbsp roasted crushed unsalted peanuts

½ red onion, finely sliced

2 ripe tomatoes, each quartered and quartered again to give 8 pieces

½ cucumber, sliced into half moons

For the dressing

1 tbsp sesame oil

juice and zest of 1 lime

1 tbsp brown sugar

1 tbsp nam pla (fish sauce)

1½ tablespoons light soy sauce

1 long red chilli (deseeded if you don't want it too spicy), finely sliced

2 garlic cloves, finely chopped

2.5cm/1in knob of fresh root ginger, peeled and grated

The weighty purple aubergines are so meaty, it even goes down well with the most carnivorous of my friends. As with most salads, you can serve it up immediately or make it in advance to let the flavours really develop. Serve on a bed of crisp lettuce.

Whisk together all the ingredients for the dressing until you have a rich glossy sauce, then set aside.

Brush each aubergine slice with a little olive oil. Heat a griddle pan until very hot, then place the aubergines on it and cook on both sides until soft and charred.

Pop the aubergine slices into a dish and mix with the herbs, peanuts, onion, tomatoes and cucumber. Drizzle with the dressing – the warm aubergine will really soak it up. Eat and enjoy the pleasant numbness the heat of it brings to your lips.

CUMIN-FRIED CHICKEN WINGS

Chicken wings are finger food at its best...

I don't even need a party to knock up a plate of these –
a night in front of the telly is occasion enough for them.
The warmth of the spices and the chillies really give them
a kick. Nibble them with an ice-cold beer – they're finger
lickin' good.

Heat the groundnut oil in a deep-fat fryer over a medium
flame.

Sift the cornflour into a large bowl or freezer bag.
Add the ground spices, lemon zest, garlic and chillies and
mix well. Toss the chicken wings in the mixture, making
sure they all have a healthy coating of the seasoned flour.
Shake off the excess flour and fry them in small batches
in the hot oil for 5 minutes until they are golden brown
and cooked through. Drain well on kitchen paper and
serve while sizzling.

SERVES 6

groundnut oil for deep-
    frying (see Cook's Notes,
    page 12)
8 tbsp cornflour
1 tbsp each of cumin seeds,
    coriander seeds and black
    peppercorns, all toasted in
    a dry pan and then ground
    to a coarse powder
½ tsp ground cinnamon
zest of 1 lemon
4 garlic cloves, crushed
2 dried red chillies, crushed
1kg/2¼lb chicken wings

PRAWN POPPADUMS

Poppadums are normally a quick filler before the main event at your local curry house, but in this recipe they are transformed into a king cracker with a topping of chilli-spiked prawn.

Fry the onion in the vegetable oil until soft. Sprinkle in the cumin and cloves and fry until the onion is golden brown. Add the tomatoes and tomato purée along with the ginger, garlic, chilli, turmeric and salt to taste and cook until the tomatoes have cooked down and are jammy – this should take about 8 minutes.

Add the prawns and stir-fry for 3–4 minutes or until they are cooked through. Take the pan off the heat, add the lime juice and stir the coconut through. Allow to cool for a few minutes, then heap a little of the mixture onto each poppadum. Garnish with the chopped coriander and extra coconut and serve.

MAKES 40

1 small onion, finely chopped
2 tbsp vegetable oil
1 tsp cumin seeds
¼ tsp crushed cloves
3 large tomatoes, chopped
1 tbsp tomato purée
2.5cm/1in knob of fresh root ginger, peeled and grated
3 garlic cloves, finely chopped
1 large red chilli (deseeded if you don't want it too spicy), chopped
½ tsp turmeric
sea salt
350g/12oz raw tiger prawns, peeled and deveined
juice of ½ lime
3 tbsp unsweetened desiccated coconut, plus 1 tbsp for garnish
40 mini poppadums
2 tbsp chopped fresh coriander

FISH FRY

If fried fish with a crisp golden exterior and a steamy, moist interior is what you crave, then look no further than this recipe.

500g/1lb 2oz any firm-fleshed fish fillets, such as pollack, cod, salmon or monkfish, cut into 2.5cm/1in cubes
groundnut oil for deep-frying (see Cook's Notes, page 12)
lime wedges, to serve

For the marinade
3 garlic cloves, crushed
5cm/2in knob of fresh root ginger, peeled and grated
1 red chilli (deseeded if you don't want it too spicy), chopped
1 tsp sea salt
juice of 1 lemon or lime

For the batter
150g/5oz gram flour
2 tbsp rice flour
½ tsp baking powder
2 tsp mango powder (amchur, see page 32)
½ tsp sea salt
1 tsp chilli powder
½ tsp turmeric
1 tbsp chopped fresh coriander leaves
1 tsp carom seeds
300ml/10fl oz water

The batter here is seasoned with chilli, carom seeds and fresh coriander leaves, as it is all over India, so as not to waste any opportunity to inject flavour.

Combine all the ingredients for the marinade in a bowl or freezer bag and then throw in the fish, stirring it around to make sure it gets well coated. Leave to soak up the flavours for at least 1 hour.

For the batter, sift the gram flour, rice flour, baking powder and mango powder into a large mixing bowl. Add the salt, chilli powder, turmeric, coriander leaves and carom seeds. Whisk in the water, a little at a time, until you have a smooth batter with the consistency of thin but creamy yoghurt.

Heat the groundnut oil in a deep-fat fryer over a high heat. Once it's sizzling, turn down the heat to medium. Dip the fish in the batter and deep-fry for 4–5 minutes until the batter is crisp and golden.

Serve with wedges of lime.

SPICY CASHEWS

These are absurdly easy to make and really hit the mark when you have a roomful of guests with the munchies.

Store them in an airtight container and they will last for week – that is, if you can resist them.

Put the sea salt and black peppercorns into a pestle and mortar and pound to a fine powder. Sprinkle in the cinnamon and pound again, then add the mango powder and chilli powder and pound.

Melt the butter in a large frying pan over a low heat and fry the cashews in batches until golden. Drain on kitchen paper. Once they have all been fried, put them back into the frying pan and sprinkle with the spice mix. Toss the cashews well, making sure they are all evenly coated with the hot spice mix.

½ tsp sea salt
1 tsp black peppercorns
¼ tsp ground cinnamon
1 tsp mango powder
  (amchur, see page 32)
1 tsp red chilli powder
25g/1oz unsalted butter
500g/1lb 2oz natural cashew
  nuts

SPICY BREADED LAMB CUTLETS

Chewing on these sweet crunchy chops is just the thing to keep your guests' tongues wagging and their appetites going.

SERVES 4

5 garlic cloves, crushed

5cm/2in knob of fresh root ginger, peeled and grated

juice of ½ lemon

1 tsp each of cumin seeds, coriander seeds and black peppercorns, all toasted in a dry pan and then ground to a coarse powder

8 small lamb cutlets, fat trimmed off and bone exposed

olive oil for shallow-frying

2 eggs

200g/7oz white breadcrumbs seasoned with sea salt (panko breadcrumbs are brilliant, but ordinary ones will do)

These are heavenly eaten hot or cold. You can find panko breadcrumbs in oriental foodstores – they give a wonderful crunch.

Put the garlic, ginger, lemon juice and ground spices into a food processor and blitz to a fine paste, then smear all over the lamb cutlets. Leave to marinate for at least 2 hours or overnight.

Heat 1cm/½in of olive oil in a frying pan. Meanwhile, beat the eggs in a bowl and pour the breadcrumbs onto a plate. Dip each cutlet in the egg and then roll it in the breadcrumbs, turning to coat well. Fry in the olive oil for 3 minutes on each side until the breadcrumbs are golden and the lamb is pink inside. Drain on kitchen paper.

TANDOORI PANEER SKEWERS

For a lipsmackingly good, meat-free feast, rustle up these paneer kebabs.

Paneer is a silken Indian cottage cheese, rather like tofu, that accommodates other flavours extremely well, and still holds its shape in fierce heat, making it ideal for barbecuing, grilling or frying.

To make the marinade, put the chillies, garlic, ginger and coriander into a food processor and blitz to a fine paste. Pour in the yoghurt and whiz again. Empty the mixture into a large mixing bowl and stir in the tomato purée, paprika, garam masala and cumin. Season to taste, pour in the lemon juice and stir again. Toss the paneer and vegetables in the marinade and leave for at least 1 hour for the paneer to soak up all the flavours. Meanwhile, soak 15 skewers in water.

When you are ready to cook, preheat the grill to medium. Thread the vegetables and paneer alternately on the skewers and grill until golden and slightly charred, turning and basting with melted butter as you go. Sprinkle with the chaat masala or mango powder to serve.

KITCHEN-ADE

To make the paneer extra soft and melt in the mouth, my sister Charon Chawla recommends laying the chopped paneer in a Pyrex dish and adding water to cover the cheese by 1cm/½in. Put the dish into the microwave and heat on a reheating setting for 1 minute. Drain well before marinating.

MAKES 15

500g/1lb 2oz paneer, cut into 2cm/¾in cubes
20 small shallots, peeled and halved, or 2 red onions, cut into wedges
1 green and 1 red pepper, each deseeded and cut into large chunks
30g/generous 1oz melted unsalted butter
2 tsp chaat masala or mango powder (amchur, see page 32)

For the marinade

2 green chillies (deseeded if you don't want it too spicy)
5 garlic cloves
1 thumb of fresh root ginger
1 handful of fresh coriander
200g/7oz thick set natural yoghurt
1 tbsp tomato purée
1 tsp paprika
2 tsp garam masala
1 tbsp ground cumin
sea salt and freshly ground black pepper
juice of ½ lemon

CHAPTER SEVEN

Hangover food

For the morning after the night before

There you are, at a college drinking session, necking the cheap pink wine – thinking it's the height of sophistication. A few sips make you giggly, a few more and you're a sex kitten, a few glasses and you've met your nemesis. After a night of cuddling the toilet rather than the dashing boy from the year above, all you were left with was a pounding headache.

Ten years on, nothing's changed that much really. You still drink pink wine – cheap or otherwise. The only real difference now is that you stop to swirl and sniff the wine – because you think that's sophisticated.

So here's the only good thing to come of drunken nights out – hangover food. And here's the secret – you don't even need be hungover to enjoy it.

BREAKFAST BURRITOS WITH CHORIZO & SCRAMBLED EGGS

The spicy sausage in these eggs is just the thing to perk you up after a night of debauchery.

SERVES 4

200g/7oz uncooked chorizo
    sausage
2 tbsp vegetable oil
8 large eggs
1 handful of chopped fresh
    coriander
4 tortilla wraps

The heat in the spices really gives your body a jump-start and is a great tonic for soothing those splintered nerves.

Slice the chorizo so they are as wide as a pound coin. Heat the vegetable oil and fry the chorizo over a medium heat until crisp and brown. Whisk the eggs together in a bowl and pour over the sausage – there is no need to season with salt or pepper since the chorizo has plenty. Let the eggs set slightly, then start stirring for big fluffy flakes of egg. Stir in the coriander.

Divide the eggs between four warmed tortillas and kiss goodbye to that hangover.

PANKO-COATED CHAMP CAKES WITH CRISPY PANCETTA

Where iron willpower fails to get you out of bed, the lure of a hearty breakfast certainly will.

If you've been out on an epic bender, you'll have no doubt woken up feeling a little tender. These comforting creamy champ cakes and salty rashers of bacon are just the thing to blow life into a foggy head. Wake-up! After all, you snooze, you lose.

Boil the unpeeled potatoes in plenty of salted water for about 20 minutes. Meanwhile, simmer the spring onions in the milk until they have softened.

Once the potatoes are tender all the way through, drain them and, when they are cool enough to handle, peel. Mash them together with the spring onions, milk and butter until you have a smooth creamy mash with no lumps. (At this stage I sometimes add a tablespoon of mustard or horseradish, but you can just stick to plain salt and pepper if you like.)

Once the mixture has cooled enough to handle, take a golf ball-size ball of it, roll in your hand and then flatten to resemble a patty. Repeat until you have about 10 potato cakes. Heat 1cm/½in of olive oil in a frying pan until medium hot. Beat the eggs in a bowl and pour the breadcrumbs onto a plate. Dip each patty in the beaten egg and then turn in the breadcrumbs to coat. Fry on both sides until golden and crisp, then drain the patties on kitchen paper. Serve with crispy pancetta and a squirt of ketchup.

MAKES 10

6 floury potatoes, such as King Edwards
100g/3½oz chopped spring onions
250ml/8fl oz full-fat milk
50g/2oz unsalted butter
1 tbsp mustard or horseradish (optional)
olive oil for shallow-frying
2 eggs
200g/7oz panko breadcrumbs (see page 80)
sea salt and freshly ground black pepper
crispy pancetta and tomato ketchup, to serve

FULL ENGLISH STACKER

Feeling a little groggy? This is the ultimate way to get over a hangover, and it goes far beyond the usual Alka Seltzer.

SERVES 2

4 good-quality sausages
4 rashers of bacon
2 portobello mushrooms
sea salt and freshly ground
    black pepper
2 small stalks of cherry
    tomatoes on the vine
olive oil and balsamic
    vinegar, to drizzle
4 thick slices of bread
1 tbsp vegetable oil for frying
2 large eggs
butter for spreading
ketchup, mustard, or brown
    sauce, to serve

Heat a griddle pan until hot. The sausages take the longest to cook, so start them off first. Place them on the hot griddle and lightly brown them all over, then turn the heat right down and cook for another 10 minutes, turning them every few minutes. Once the bacon goes into the pan, the sausages will need another 5 minutes – they should be sticky and dark brown by the time you've finished.

Once the sausages have been cooking for about 10 minutes, turn up the heat to medium and lay the bacon in the pan, together with the mushrooms, stalk-side up. Cook the bacon for 3–4 minutes on each side – depending on how crispy you want it. Cook the mushrooms for 2 minutes on one side, season with black pepper and a little sea salt and then turn and cook for a further 4 minutes.

Drizzle the tomatoes with olive oil and a little balsamic vinegar and season with plenty of salt and pepper. Place on the griddle and cook for 5 minutes.

When everything is almost cooked, toast the bread and get ready to fry your eggs. Heat the vegetable oil in a frying pan. When it's hot, gently break the eggs into it. Let them set for 30 seconds, then lower the heat and continue to cook them, basting the tops by flicking the hot fat over. They'll be cooked after about 1 minute, but if you prefer the yolk well set, leave them in the pan for a little longer.

Butter the toast. To assemble the stacker, balance the mushroom and bacon on one slice of toast, cover with another slice of toast, buttered-side up, and place the sausages and egg on it, then top with the tomatoes. Serve with ketchup, mustard or brown sauce – or all three if your head is really banging!

CHEDDAR & SAUSAGE MUFFINS

If breakfast means more to you than just a soggy bowl of insipid cereal, you'll adore these muffins.

MAKES 12

275g/9½oz plain flour
1 heaped tsp baking powder
1 tsp sea salt
2–3 heaped tsp English
    mustard powder
2 large eggs
225ml/7½fl oz full-fat milk
125g/4oz grated Cheddar or
    Gruyère cheese
225g/8oz pork sausages,
    fried and sliced
leaves stripped from a few
    sprigs of thyme

They're my idea of perfect Sunday afternoon baking, if only to shoo away those Monday morning blues. They're especially good if Sunday afternoon domestic goddess-hood turns into Sunday evening indulging!

Preheat the oven to 190°C/375°F/gas 5. Line a 12-hole muffin tin with muffin cases.

Sift the flour and baking powder into a large bowl and add the salt and mustard powder. Mix well.

Whisk together 1 egg and the milk and pour it into the flour. Fold in the cheese, sausages and thyme leaves. Don't go stir crazy and over-mix it – it should be lumpy and textured. Spoon the mixture generously into the muffin cases. Beat the second egg and brush over the muffins with a pastry brush to give them a mellow golden glaze.

Bake the muffins for 15–20 minutes until they are cooked through. They are lovely eaten hot or cold.

SMOKED SALMON CROQUE

Here's the hangover cure for the squiffy sophisticat – I'll drink to that.

Whoever said sophisticated wine doesn't give you a hangover was a big fat liar, and now you know 'cause you too were duped. But then again, you did drink an estate's worth of the good stuff.

Brush 2 slices of bread with melted butter on one side only. Spread 1 teaspoon of mustard on the unbuttered side of one slice, then add a little rocket, followed by a slice of smoked salmon. Season with pepper and squeeze on a little lemon juice, then top with a generous amount of cheese and the remaining slice of bread, unbuttered-side down.

Heat a griddle pan over a medium heat. When it is hot, lay the sandwich on it, cheese-side down. Griddle for 5 minutes, then turn it over and griddle for another 2 minutes. Repeat with the remaining bread. Slice into diagonal halves and enjoy with a cup of Earl Grey tea.

MAKES 4

8 slices of sandwich loaf
20g/³⁄₄oz melted unsalted
    butter
4 tsp Dijon mustard
30g/generous 1oz wild rocket
150g/5oz smoked salmon
freshly ground black pepper
juice of ½ lemon
100g/3½oz Gruyère cheese

SMOKED SALMON, SPINACH & SCRAMBLED EGG BAGELS
WITH HOLLANDAISE SAUCE

This is my favourite breakfast and, yes, that probably has a lot to do with the heavy butter content, but look – it hasn't done the French any harm!

Cooking it for friends makes me feel grown up and sophisticated and, let's face it, once you have got a forkful of hollandaise sauce in your mouth, nothing in life ever seems so bad.

SERVES 4

4 bagels, each split in two
200g/7oz smoked salmon

**For the perfect
scrambled eggs**
8 eggs
25g/1oz unsalted butter
1 dessertspoon crème fraîche
I tbsp chopped fresh chives
generous seasoning of sea salt and freshly
　　ground black pepper

For the spinach
1 knob of unsalted butter
250g/9oz baby leaf spinach
freshly grated nutmeg

For the hollandaise
2 egg yolks
1½ tbsp lemon juice
1½ tbsp white wine vinegar
125g/4oz unsalted butter
a dash of cayenne pepper

As with most breakfasts, this is all about timing. My advice is to tackle the hollandaise sauce first. It has a reputation as a tricky sauce, but it's really quite simple as long as you stick to the rules. Put the egg yolks, lemon juice and vinegar into an electric mixer and blend. Melt the butter in a pan over a low heat – it must not burn. As soon as it is bubbling, take off the heat and put into a jug ready to pour over the eggs. This is the bit where virgin hollandaisers can go wrong, so pay attention! The trick is to pour the butter in oh-so-slowly while mixing, which is why it's important to pour from a jug and not your saucepan – you have far more control. Keep pouring the butter into the egg mixture in a slow steady trickle and eventually you should be left with a thick, delicious, lickable creamy sauce. Stir in the cayenne pepper and salt and pepper to taste.

Now for the spinach – this is a 1-minute job. Melt the butter in a pan and add the spinach – it should take about 1 minute to wilt. Season with the nutmeg – job done.

Get your bagels in the toaster and make the eggs. Beat the eggs, but don't season at all – putting salt in them at this stage makes them watery and rubbery. Melt the butter in a pan and throw in the eggs. Let them almost set, as you would when making an omelette, and then start stirring to get gorgeous flakes of scramble. When they are just a little runny, mix in the crème fraîche, chives and salt and pepper to taste – the perfect scrambled eggs!

Now get ready to assemble your breakfast bagel. Lay the bagels on a plate, top with the wilted spinach, smoked salmon and eggs and, finally, drizzle with hollandaise sauce. Gobble up immediately.

SMOKED MACKEREL TOASTIES

This simple, delicious, omega- and iron-rich sandwich will have you feeling human in no time.

SERVES 4

200g/7oz smoked mackerel
2 tbsp horseradish sauce
2 tbsp crème fraîche
juice of ½ lemon
sea salt and freshly ground
    black pepper
1 generous handful of
    watercress
butter for spreading
8 slices of thick sandwich
    loaf

A raw egg swallowed whole. A plate of chips and 12 cans of coke. Raw fish and a strawberry doughnut. The hair of the dog. Don't believe the hype. Some people will embrace anything to fend off a full-blown hangover, but these so-called cures aren't tasty or sensible and, let's face it, you've suffered enough.

Flake the mackerel, then combine it with the horseradish, crème fraîche, lemon juice and seasoning. Tear the watercress and mix it in too.

Butter two slices of bread on one side, then layer the filling onto the unbuttered side of one slice and place the other slice, unbuttered-side down, on top. Repeat with the remaining bread and grill in a sandwich toaster until golden.

APPLE & GRANOLA MUFFINS

If you've lost your fizz, wash these tasty muffins down with a double espresso. You'll have bubbled back to life by the time you hit the office.

Preheat the oven to 180°C/350°F/gas 4. Line a 12-hole muffin tin with muffin cases.

Whisk together the yoghurt, eggs, olive oil, lemon juice and zest until you have a thick batter.

In another bowl, sift the flour into a bowl (tip any kernels left in the sieve in too) and stir in the brown sugar, then mix until the sugar is well incorporated. Sprinkle in the granola, cinnamon and salt and give it another mix. Finally, stir in the chopped apple, making sure it is well coated with the flour. Stir this mixture into the egg batter. You should be left with a thick sticky dough.

Spoon the batter into the muffin cases and bake for 25 minutes until they are cooked through. Leave to cool and eat cold.

MAKES 12

175g/6oz natural yoghurt
2 large eggs
2 tbsp olive oil
1 tbsp lemon juice
grated zest of 1 lemon
300g/10oz wholewheat
    self-raising flour
150g/5oz brown sugar
150g/5oz granola
1 tsp ground cinnamon
½ tsp sea salt
1 Bramley apple,
    chopped into 5mm/
    ¼ in pieces

EXOTIC SYRUPY FRUIT SALAD
WITH TEMPURA BRIOCHE

There is something so satisfying about eating this chilled fruit salad with the hot, almost pancake-like, fried brioche.

When I've been really good I allow myself a scoop of vanilla ice cream to go with it too. Make the fruit salad the night before – it gives time for the fruit to really soak up the flavours of the syrup.

SERVES 6

1 small pineapple, cut into chunks
1 hard-fleshed mango, cut into chunks
1 guava, cut into chunks
20 lychees, stoned
1 Chinese pear, cut into chunks
1 small papaya, cut into chunks
Greek yoghurt or vanilla ice cream,
   to serve

For the syrup
4 tbsp golden caster sugar
zest of 1 lime
a few sprigs of fresh mint
1cm/½in knob of fresh root ginger

1 vanilla pod
2 star anise
200ml/7fl oz water

For the tempura brioche
groundnut oil for deep-frying
   (see Cook's Notes, page 12)
50g/2oz plain flour
50g/2oz cornflour
1 tbsp baking powder
½ tsp ground cinnamon
1 egg, beaten
200ml/7fl oz ice-cold mineral
   water
1 ice cube
8 slices from a brioche loaf

To make the syrup, tip the sugar, lime zest, mint, ginger, vanilla pod and star anise into the water and bring to the boil. Simmer for 10 minutes, then take off the heat and cool. Once it's cooled down, strain it and pour over the prepared fruit. Pop the fruit into the refrigerator overnight or for at least 2 hours, so they have a chance to soak up all the flavours.

To prepare the tempura batter for the brioche, heat the groundnut oil in a deep-fat fryer. Sift both the flours and the baking powder into a mixing bowl, then add the cinnamon. Mix the beaten egg and water together, pour onto the flour and mix a few times – be careful not to over mix it. Add the ice cube. Dip the brioche slices into the batter, making sure they are well coated, and then deep-fry until crisp and golden.

Serve immediately with the chilled fruit salad and a dollop of Greek yoghurt or a scoop of vanilla ice cream.

FRENCH TOAST WITH BANANA, CHOCOLATE HAZELNUT SPREAD & PISTACHIOS

Suffering souls deserve a sweet treat and nothing is sweeter on a killer hangover than this.

When I'm being decadent, I use a handful of dark chocolate buttons – my favourite are Valrhona – for each sandwich instead of chocolate spread. As it cooks, the buttons melt and ooze. You are what you eat, and if you eat this you'll be sexy.

Spread two of the slices of bread with a thick gooey layer of chocolate spread or pile on the chocolate buttons. Top with a layer of bananas and then close the deal with the remaining bread.

Beat the eggs in a bowl with the sugar, milk, cinnamon and vanilla extract. Place the sandwiches in the sunny egg mixture and let them soak it up for 2 minutes on each side.

Melt the butter in a pan over a medium to low heat, then fry the sandwiches on both sides until they are golden and puffy. Serve with a scattering of pistachio nuts and a dusting of icing sugar if you absolutely must. Eat at once.

KITCHEN-ADE

Bread that is slightly stale works best for French toast, as it doesn't disintegrate when you wet it with the egg.

Cook the sandwiches over a gentle heat so that they cook all the way through and the chocolate really melts into a sticky goo.

MAKES 2 SANDWICHES

4 thick slices of white bread (see Kitchen-ade)
chocolate hazelnut spread or 150g/5oz dark chocolate buttons
2 bananas, thinly sliced
4 eggs
4 tbsp caster sugar
4 tbsp full-fat milk
1 tsp ground cinnamon
2 tsp vanilla extract
a generous knob of unsalted butter for frying
1 handful of sliced pistachio nuts
icing sugar, to dust

BANANA BUTTERMILK PANCAKES

When you're the victim of a throbbing, galloping, begging-for-mercy hangover, you need a good friend who'll come over and whip you up a stacked plate of these.

MAKES 12

300g/10oz self-raising flour
50g/2oz caster sugar
1 large banana
2 large eggs
500ml/18fl oz buttermilk
2 tbsp natural yoghurt
40g/1½oz melted unsalted
    butter, plus extra for
    frying
a generous grating of fresh
    nutmeg
strawberries, to serve

**For the butterscotch
sauce**

200g/7oz caster sugar
300ml/10fl oz double cream

The pounding in your head will turn into sweet birdsong with just one treacly spoonful.

Dear kind friend,

Make the butterscotch sauce by melting the sugar in a pan. When it's a light amber liquid, whisk in the double cream. Easy – there's nothing more to it than that.

Now for the pancakes. Combine the flour and sugar in a bowl. In a separate bowl, mash the banana until it looks like baby food and then beat in the eggs, buttermilk and yoghurt. Whisk this into the flour and pour in the melted butter, then add a good grating of nutmeg.

Heat a frying pan over a medium heat. Brush the surface with a little melted butter and then pour a ladleful of the batter into the centre of the pan. Fry for 1 minute on each side. Remove from the pan and repeat with the remaining batter. As they come out of the pan, stack each cooked pancake between layers of greaseproof paper.

Stack two or three pancakes together, pile with hulled strawberries and butterscotch sauce and carry on a tray to your best friend's bedside. Bask in the glory of your good deed and know that she'll do the same for you.

POTATO PARATHAS

Parathas are India's answer to the greasy spoon fry-up.

Of course, there are no eggs, bacon or sausages, but there is still the seductive sizzle of something hissing in a pan. Just as the scent of cooking bacon breaks the will of hardened vegetarians everywhere, the aroma of fried parathas is known for bringing the most devoted dieter to her knees. Traditionally, these are fried in ghee or clarified butter, but I try to keep them relatively healthy by cooking them in vegetable or olive oil. Still, if it's authenticity you seek, be prepared to count a few extra calories.

To prepare the dough, combine the chapatti flour with the olive oil and salt. Pour in enough water to make a smooth firm dough, then knead well, until it is springy and elastic. Leave it aside to rest while you make the filling.

Boil the potatoes until they are tender, but still have a little bite – about 15 minutes. When they are cool enough to handle, peel and grate them and then mix in the onion, chillies, cumin, carom seeds, salt and coriander. Divide the potato stuffing into 5 equal portions.

Knead the dough again and divide it into 10 equal balls. Roll two of the balls into large thin circles, dusting as you roll with a little flour to stop them sticking. Spread one portion of the potato mix thinly over the surface of one circle and top with the second one – just as though you were making a sandwich. Press down firmly to make sure the two halves adhere well.

Grease a flat-bottomed frying pan with 1 teaspoon of vegetable oil and heat until very hot. Place a paratha in the pan, lower the heat and leave for a couple of minutes to cook. Brush a layer of oil on the top side and then flip over and cook for a further 2 minutes until golden brown and crispy. Repeat with the remaining parathas, adding more vegetable oil as necessary.

MAKES 5

For the dough

400g/14oz chapatti flour,
    plus a little extra to dust
3 tbsp olive oil
1 tsp sea salt
about 200ml/7fl oz water
vegetable oil for frying
ghee for greasing

For the filling

2 large potatoes
1 red onion, finely chopped
2 green chillies (deseeded if
    you don't want it too
    spicy), finely chopped
1 tsp cumin seeds
½ tsp carom seeds
½ tsp sea salt
1 small handful of fresh
    coriander, finely chopped

To serve

Indian mango or lemon
    pickle
natural yoghurt

MASALA OMELETTE

When you're whimpering with a cloudy-headed, fuzzy-tongued hangover, this omelette is just the prescription.

SERVES 1

1 tablespoon vegetable oil
½ small red onion, finely chopped
1 tsp cumin
1 green chilli (deseeded if you don't want it too spicy), finely chopped
1 small tomato, chopped
2 eggs
½ tsp garam masala
sea salt and freshly ground black pepper
1 tbsp chopped fresh coriander
bread or warmed pitta bread and chilli sauce, to serve

The chilli will really make you sweat out all those nasty toxins and leave you feeling 100 per cent better, without a chalky headache tablet in sight.

Preheat the grill to hot. Heat the vegetable oil in a non-stick frying pan and fry the onion, cumin and chilli until soft. Stir in the tomato and fry for another minute.

Meanwhile, beat the eggs and season with the garam masala, salt and pepper. Whisk in the coriander. Pour the beaten eggs into the frying pan and tilt the pan, so that the egg sets evenly. Once it has set underneath, pop it under the grill until it's just set on top. Serve stuffed in bread or warmed pitta bread with a dollop of chilli sauce.

ONION & CUMIN HASH BROWNS
WITH FRIED EGGS

The aftermath of a night on the tiles can be messy. But along with the regretful, eye-watering symptoms, you can also look forward to a tasty pick-me-up.

When you have a plate of these spiky hash browns and glorious wobbly eggs in front of you, you can't possibly have any morning-after regrets. And besides – if you don't have a hangover, you didn't have a good time.

Soak the grated potatoes in cold water for extra crunch. Drain, then squeeze out as much excess water as possible. Put into a large bowl with the onion, coriander, chilli and cumin seeds and mix well, then fold in the flour and beat in the egg.

Heat 1 tablespoon of olive oil in a non-stick frying pan. With wet hands, shape 2 tablespoons of the potato mixture into a flat fritter and cook over a medium heat for about 3 minutes on each side until golden brown and crispy. Drain on kitchen paper. Repeat with the remaining mixture, adding more olive oil as necessary. Serve 3 per person and top each serving with a fried egg.

MAKES 12

500g/1lb 2oz peeled and grated potatoes, such as Desiree
1 small red onion, grated
4 tbsp chopped fresh coriander
1 green chilli (deseeded if you don't want it too spicy), finely chopped
2 tsp cumin seeds
1 heaped tbsp plain flour
1 egg, lightly beaten
olive oil for frying
4 fried eggs, to serve

CHAPTER EIGHT

Hard-up food

*For when you've spent all your
lolly on your Louboutins*

There was one sentiment my fashionable friends related to more than anything in *Sex and the City*. Carrie Bradshaw, wide-eyed and stylish, turns to her friends and says, 'When I first moved to New York and was totally broke, I used to buy *Vogue* instead of dinner; I felt it fed me more.' It seems to me that Carrie had turned her kitchen storecupboard into a walk-in wardrobe. Even if your vice, like Carrie's, is spending on vertiginous shoes what most people spend on rent, you can still eat well.

Being frugal is the new fashion. Open up your storecupboard, dust down that tin of sardines you thought would never see the light of day and get cooking. You needn't suffer for the sake of fashion. You can have your Louboutins and live well on a shoestring budget.

Chow down – give yourself a cheap thrill.

ZESTY ANGEL HAIR SPAGHETTI
WITH GARLIC, CHILLI, LEMON AND OLIVE OIL

Pasta is as thrifty as it gets, but it needn't taste cheap.

SERVES 4–6

400g/14oz angel hair
    spaghetti
sea salt
150ml/5fl oz olive oil
1 long red chilli (deseeded if
    you don't want it too
    spicy), finely sliced
4–6 garlic cloves, finely
    sliced
zest and juice of 1 lemon
freshly grated Parmesan
    cheese, to serve

Buy the best pasta you can afford and, as long as you cook it perfectly al dente, you won't feel like you're eating on a budget. You really can't put a price on the pleasure you'll get from eating a bowl of blonde spaghetti like this, dressed with a dazzling lemon and garlic oil.

Boil the pasta in plenty of boiling salted water until al dente.

Meanwhile, pour the olive oil into a pan and put it over a low heat. Add the chilli and garlic and heat slowly until the garlic turns a pale gold. Add the lemon zest and juice and heat for a further minute. Drain the pasta and add to the garlicky olive oil. Sprinkle Parmesan over and serve at once.

KITCHEN-ADE
If you're following packet instructions on cooking pasta, always cook it for a minute less than suggested, as the residual heat continues to cook it long after it is out of the water.

SARDINES IN SPICY TAMARIND SAUCE

Tinned sardines, even the very posh ones packed in glossy, impressive tins luxuriating in olive oil, are cheap and tasty.

When you get bored of eating them piled up on toast, try them in this Indian-inspired tamarind sauce, where they have a wealth of fragrant flavour.

Heat the vegetable oil in a pan. Once it's sizzling hot, sprinkle in the mustard seeds and then, as soon as they pop, stir in the asafoetida and scatter in the curry leaves. Stir briefly, then add the tomatoes and turmeric. Let the tomatoes stew for 5 minutes.

Pour in the tamarind, water and salt to taste and bring to a simmer. Let the sauce simmer and reduce – it should thicken and become glossier. Pile the sardines into the sauce, cover the pan and let them warm through for 5 minutes. Scatter with the coriander and serve with steamed basmati rice.

SERVES 4

1 tbsp vegetable oil
1 tsp mustard seeds
1 pinch of asafoetida
    (see Kitchen-ade)
10 curry leaves
    (see Kitchen-ade)
2 juicy ripe tomatoes, chopped
½ tsp turmeric
2 tbsp tamarind concentrate
150ml/5fl oz water
sea salt
3 × 120g tins of sardines in
    olive oil, drained
3 tbsp chopped fresh coriander
steamed basmati rice, to serve

KITCHEN-ADE

Asafoetida, alias 'devil's dung', is a spice with a strong pungent scent. Once you cook it, though, it just leaves a delicate fragrance and taste similar to that of onions and garlic. It is eaten in India as a digestive aid and also by Jains (a caste of Hindus), who do not eat onions or garlic. You're sure to find it in Indian food stores, but if you still can't get hold of it, order it online at www.spicesofindia.co.uk. This recipe won't fall apart without it, but it gives it an authentic flavour and aroma and it'll be another spice to add to your repertoire.

Packets of curry leaves are readily available in Indian and oriental food stores. Buy them fresh and then stash them in the freezer. They keep really well for weeks on end and don't lose their fragrant aroma.

CHICKPEA & POTATO CURRY

A tin of chickpeas should be compulsory in any kitchen storecupboard.

SERVES 4

4 garlic cloves, roughly
    chopped
2 red chillies (deseeded if
    you don't want it too
    spicy), roughly chopped
5cm/2in knob of fresh root
    ginger, peeled and
    roughly chopped
1 large red onion, finely
    chopped
1 tsp cumin seeds
a generous slug of olive oil
½ tsp ground cinnamon
1 tbsp tomato purée
½ × 400g tin of chopped
    tomatoes
½ tsp turmeric
1 tbsp caster sugar
1 tbsp chopped fenugreek
    leaves (optional)
sea salt
1 × 400g tin of chickpeas
1 large potato, cut into
    8 wedges
600ml/1 pint water
juice of ½ a lime
chopped fresh coriander,
    to garnish

Food snobs may balk at the idea of using a tinned variety, but I love the friendly convenience of these in their briny juices. They're perfect for beefing up salads, as a side to a platter of fish or meat, and especially celebrated as the main event in this aromatic curry.

The fenugreek isn't essential here, but I do love the pungency and depth of flavour it adds to soups and stews. I tend to buy a big bunch of it from the Indian grocer, chop it finely and store in a freezer bag in the freezer. It keeps for months and is a convenient herb to have on hand.

Put the garlic, chillies and ginger into a food processor and blitz to a paste. Fry the onion and cumin in the olive oil until golden and then add the ginger, garlic and chilli paste along with the cinnamon. Stir briefly until the spice becomes fragrant, then add the tomato purée, tomatoes, turmeric, sugar, fenugreek and salt to taste.

Stew the curry base until the tomatoes have broken down and reduced – about 5 minutes. Tumble in the chickpeas and potato and pour in the water. Cover the dish and simmer until the potatoes are tender – 12–15 minutes. Squeeze in the lime juice and top with the chopped coriander.

KITCHEN-ADE

My mother showed me how to keep coriander wonderfully fresh and, honestly, this makes it last for at least two weeks at a time. Buy a bunch of coriander – do not wash it and make sure it is dry. Wrap it up in kitchen paper – literally blanket it – and then store in the fridge in an airtight container. Wash it and use as needed.

STIR-FRY SESAME NOODLES

Noodles are as cheap, comforting and easy to cook as pasta.

These slithery ones make use of any leftover vegetables you may have lurking in your fridge or freezer, and if you eat oodles of them (and believe me, that is no task) your bank balance may creep out of the red. The perfect lunch for the credit crunch.

Simmer the noodles in a pan of boiling water for 3 minutes or according to the packet instructions. (Dried noodles have already been cooked, so need only to cook briefly to reconstitute the water.) Once they are done, drain them and refresh in cold water to stop them cooking any further, then drain again.

In a wok, heat the vegetable oil and then pour in the sesame oil. It will become fragrant almost immediately, and once it does stir-fry the vegetables – hardest ones first. So start with the carrots – cook them on a high heat for 2–3 minutes, then add the onion, pepper strips and courgette, followed by the green beans and baby corn. Finally, scatter in the ginger and curry powder, tossing well. Don't be afraid to lift your wok and throw the vegetables around – this keeps them nice and crunchy. Sling in the noodles and toss again.

Pour in the soy and sweet chilli sauces. Take the wok off the heat and finish with a squeeze of fresh lime and a smattering of sesame seeds.

SERVES 6

300g/10oz medium egg noodles
1 tbsp vegetable oil
2 tsp sesame oil
2 small carrots, thinly sliced on the diagonal
1 red onion, sliced
½ red pepper and ½ yellow pepper, deseeded and cut into thin strips
1 small courgette, trimmed and finely sliced
100g/3½oz green beans, halved
100g/3½oz baby corn, sliced in half lengthways
5cm/2in knob of fresh root ginger, peeled and cut into matchsticks
1 tsp mild Madras curry powder
2 tbsp light soy sauce
1 tbsp sweet chilli sauce
juice of ½ lime
2 tbsp toasted sesame seeds

PORTOBELLO MUSHROOM & CHEDDAR CRUMBLE

You want to sink your teeth into a sirloin, but your budget doesn't quite stretch.

SERVES 4

3 garlic cloves, thinly sliced
8 portobello mushrooms
extra virgin olive oil to
    drizzle

For the tomato sauce

2 tbsp olive oil
1 onion, finely chopped
2 fat garlic cloves, chopped
1 dried red chilli, crumbled
1 × 400g tin of chopped
    tomatoes
1 tsp caster sugar
sea salt and freshly ground
    black pepper
2 tbsp chopped fresh flat-leaf
    parsley

For the crumble

200g/7oz breadcrumbs
1 heaped tbsp chopped fresh
    flat-leaf parsley
20g/³⁄₄oz Parmesan cheese,
    finely grated
50g/2oz Cheddar cheese,
    finely grated
1 handful of torn fresh basil
    leaves

Solution? Try a mushroom instead. These magic portobellos are weighty and beefy, dripping with the kind of tender juices you only get from a good steak. Seriously – it's so much like steak you'll think you're tripping.

Preheat the oven to 190°C/375°F/gas 5. To prepare the crumble mixture, mix all the ingredients together well and season to taste. Set it aside and get on with preparing the tomato sauce.

In a frying pan, heat the olive oil and sauté the onion until soft and translucent. Add the chopped garlic and chilli and fry for 3 minutes, then add the tomatoes, sugar and seasoning. Let it bubble away on a low heat for 15–20 minutes. Add a little bit of water if it gets too thick – it should have a pouring consistency. Finally, stir in the parsley.

Peel and trim the mushrooms. Spread half the tomato sauce over the base of a large roasting tin, then top with the sliced garlic and mushrooms, stalk-side up. Pour the rest of the sauce over and top with the crumble. Drizzle with some extra virgin olive oil and bake in the oven for 20 minutes until it's bubbling on top. Serve with a simple rocket salad.

DHAL KEEMA

There's no need to head to the fancy-schmancy wallet-swashing Indian restaurant when you crave some spicy indulgence.

SERVES 6

3 tbsp vegetable oil
1 onion, finely chopped
1 tsp cumin
3cm/1¼in knob of fresh
    root ginger, peeled and
    grated
4 garlic cloves, chopped
½ tsp cloves, crushed
2 dried red chillies,
    crumbled
4 green cardamom pods,
    crushed
1 cinnamon stick
1 bay leaf
½ tsp turmeric
200ml/7fl oz chopped
    tinned tomatoes
450g/1lb good-quality lean
    minced lamb
100ml/3½fl oz water
100g/3½oz Bengal gram,
    soaked in cold water for
    2 hours
naan or flat bread to serve

This tasty lamb and lentil curry is quick and easy enough to do at home, and is kind to your purse too.

Heat the vegetable oil in a pan and sauté the onion with the cumin until soft and golden brown. The cumin adds a wonderfully nutty, earthy note here. Add the ginger and garlic and fry again for 2 minutes.

Sprinkle in the cloves, chillies, cardamoms, cinnamon stick, bay leaf and turmeric and fry for 2 minutes. The spices will really perfume your kitchen. Pour in the tomatoes and stew until they are thick and jammy. Now stir in the mince, making sure it gets a good coating of all the spice mix. Stir-fry for a few minutes to seal it, then pour in the water. Cover the pan and cook for 15 minutes.

Drain the Bengal gram and stir into the pan, then cover the pan again and cook for another 5 minutes. Finally, take the lid off and cook the mince over a high heat to dry off any excess moisture – it should be moist but not watery. Serve with quilts of doughy naan or any other flat bread.

BAKED POLLACK WITH TOMATO & OLIVE SAUCE

With all the scares of cod being so scarce, I have been trying to use alternatives, and I have to say pollack is the closest you'll get to cod.

Added to this, it's much cheaper. I promise no one but you will know the difference.

Preheat the oven to 190°C/375°F/gas 5. To make the tomato and olive sauce, fry the onion and garlic in the olive oil until golden and then break in the chilli and oregano. Pour in the tomatoes, add the sugar and stew until slightly thickened. Throw in the olives and mix once. Season with salt and pepper and pour into a baking tray.

Season the fish fillets with plenty of salt and pepper and place on the tomato sauce. Squeeze the lemon juice over and then crown each fillet with a sugared lemon slice. Bake in the oven for about 12 minutes until the fish is beautifully opaque. Sprinkle with some fresh basil or flat-leaf parsley, if you have any to hand, and dress with a drizzle of extra virgin olive oil.

SERVES 4

1 red onion, finely chopped
3 garlic cloves, chopped
1 tbsp olive oil
1 dried red chilli
1 tsp dried oregano
1 × 400g tin of chopped
    tomatoes
1 tsp caster sugar
12 kalamata olives
sea salt and freshly ground
    black pepper
4 fillets of pollack, 175g/6oz
    each
juice of 1 lemon
4 lemon slices dipped in
    sugar
chopped fresh basil leaves or
    flat-leaf parsley, to garnish
    (optional)
extra virgin olive oil, to
    drizzle

NASI GORENG

Make a meal of leftover rice...

This devilishly spicy, fried rice recipe is one more cheap trick from the box of the frugal foodie trying to save for *yet another* pair of shoes.

Put the onion, garlic, chillies and anchovies into a food processor along with the shrimp paste and salt and pulse until you have a smooth paste. Fry the paste in 3 tablespoons of the vegetable oil for 8–10 minutes, stirring constantly to cook out the raw ingredients. When the paste turns a deep shade of crimson, toss in the prawns and stir-fry for 2 minutes. Add the green beans and cook again for another minute. Fold in the rice and stir well, making sure the paste and prawns are evenly distributed. Push the rice to one side of the pan and then pour in the beaten eggs. When they just begin to set, stir to scramble them and push into the rice.

In a separate pan, heat the remaining oil and fry the whole egg until the white is puffy and crisp at the edges and the yolk is gloriously runny.

Serve a mountain of rice on a plate, scattered with the spring onions for extra crunch and a squeeze of lime juice, and the fried egg balanced victoriously on the summit.

SERVES 4

1 onion, roughly chopped
4 garlic cloves, roughly chopped
2 red chillies (deseeded if you don't want it too spicy), roughly chopped
6–8 anchovies in olive oil, drained and roughly chopped
1 tsp shrimp paste
1 tsp sea salt
4 tbsp vegetable oil
125g/4oz raw tiger prawns, peeled and deveined
100g/3½oz green beans, chopped
600g/1lb 5oz cooked rice
3 beaten eggs, plus 1 whole egg
3 spring onions, sliced
juice of ½ lime

SPICY SAUSAGE RAGU BAKE

This bake is a clever way of using good-quality sausages and making them go that little bit further.

SERVES 6

2 tbsp olive oil

100g/3½oz diced pancetta or bacon

1 red onion, finely chopped

3 celery sticks, finely chopped

1 carrot, chopped

leaves stripped from 3 sprigs of thyme

2 garlic cloves, chopped

½ tsp chilli flakes

200g/7oz chestnut mushrooms, sliced

6 Italian sausages, taken out of their cases

200ml/7fl oz red wine

1 × 400g tin of chopped tomatoes

sea salt and freshly ground black pepper

500g/1lb 2oz penne or rigatoni

100g/3½oz mozzarella cheese, grated

100g/3½oz Parmesan cheese, grated

Being frugal shouldn't mean you skip out on quality. Cheap sausages hardly contain any meat at all – by law they only have to have 40 per cent meat and even that is sometimes made up of gristly old fat. This bake is as tasty and comforting as a lasagne without all the pfaffy layering. Not such a silly sausage after all!

Heat the olive oil in a pan and then sauté the pancetta or bacon, the onion, celery and carrot until the pancetta is golden and the vegetables have coloured and softened. Add a little thyme, the garlic, chilli flakes and mushrooms and crumble in the sausage meat. Fry for 6–8 minutes, then pour in the wine and let the alcohol bubble and evaporate. Stir in the tomatoes and seasoning, then simmer the sauce for 15 minutes.

Meanwhile, cook the pasta in plenty of boiling salted water until al dente. Preheat the oven to 190°C/375°F/ gas 5.

Drain the pasta and then stir it into the sauce. Pour the pasta and sauce into a baking dish and top with the two cheeses. Bake in the oven for 15–20 minutes until the cheese has crisped up on top.

LEFT-OVER ROAST CHICKEN PAELLA

One man's carcass is another man's meat.

I love and treasure my well-worn copy of Simon Hopkinson's *Roast Chicken and Other Stories*. I adore his honest recipes – but it always made me wonder: whatever happened to the leftovers? In my story, a prudent princess in Balenciaga boots turns the sad flesh clinging onto the skinny carcass into a sumptuous and cheap paella. Everyone in the kingdom ate and was merry (oh, I do love a happy ending!). The moral of the story? Waste not, want not.

Heat the olive oil in a pan, then fry the onion until soft and pale. Throw in the tomatoes and garlic and fry for another 5 minutes until they have broken down. Add the chicken and stir for 1 minute, then mix in the rice. Pour in the stock and mix again, then pour the saffron into the rice. Let the water come up to the boil, then lower the heat, cover the pan and simmer for 10–15 minutes.

Add the peas, roasted pepper and parsley, season with salt and cook for a further 5 minutes, then serve.

SERVES 6

30ml/1fl oz olive oil
1 onion, finely chopped
2 tomatoes, finely chopped
2 garlic cloves, chopped
300g/10oz cooked chicken, cut into bite-sized pieces
350g/12oz long-grain rice
800ml/scant 1½ pints chicken stock
1 generous pinch of saffron strands pounded in a little warm water
150g/5oz peas
1 roasted red pepper (from a jar), sliced
1 handful of finely chopped fresh flat-leaf parsley
sea salt

CHAPTER NINE

Skinny food

For when you feel the pinch of the Chloe jeans

Slimming shakes, water that makes you thin, pills that melt fat, soups that shift cellulite – I've been a sucker for all of these. Until pulling your weight (admittedly sometimes a heavy one to pull) becomes as easy as gobbling up a tray of chocolate truffles, we'll always look for the next miracle weight-loss fad. Sadly, the more we obsess, the more we fantasise about food dipped in fat.

The fall off the diet wagon is a hard one. I don't know any woman who hasn't sat there, crazy-eyed in the moonlight, frozen chocolate dessert in one hand and spoon held like a spade in the other!

Don't despair. Put down the spoon and step away from the refrigerator. I repeat – step away from the refrigerator! Study the following chapter. Waistline-friendly food can still be tasty – see?

THAI PAPAYA SALAD WITH PRAWNS

This salad captures everything Thai food should be: hot, sweet, sour and salty all at once – a sensational pleasure on the tongue.

SERVES 4–6

1 green papaya, halved and
    deseeded
100g/3½oz green beans
200g/7oz ready-to-eat
    jumbo king prawns
1 tbsp lightly toasted peanuts

For the dressing

2 garlic cloves
2 Thai chillies, deseeded
3 tbsp nam pla (fish sauce)
juice of 2 limes
1 heaped tsp brown sugar
12–15 cherry tomatoes,
    halved

Green papayas can be hard to come by, but head to an oriental store and they should be in plentiful supply.

Begin by peeling and grating the green papaya. Use a shredder or a Chinese mandolin, if you have one, otherwise just stick to a regular cheese grater. Soak the grated flesh in cold water for about 5 minutes and then drain thoroughly. This will help keep it extra crunchy.

Cut the beans into thirds. Blanch in boiling water for 3 minutes, then drain and refresh in cold water – again, this will keep them crispy and stop their retained heat from overcooking them. Drain again.

For the dressing, smash the garlic and chillies in a large pestle and mortar and then pour in the fish sauce and lime juice. Mix in the sugar and add the tomatoes, bruising them lightly so that their juices run into the dressing.

Pour the contents of the mortar over the shredded papaya and throw in the green beans and prawns. Crush the peanuts and sprinkle over. Mix well and enjoy the blissful balance of hot, sweet, salty and sour!

MANGO RICE & CRAYFISH SALAD

The sprightly dressing is so yummy, you won't even feel like you've missed out.

SERVES 4

150g/5oz brown rice
sea salt
200g/7oz crayfish tails,
    cooked and peeled
1 small Lebanese cucumber,
    diced
4 spring onions, chopped
1 large firm mango, peeled
    and diced
1 bunch of coriander,
    chopped
2 tbsp toasted peanuts

For the dressing

75ml/3fl oz light coconut
    milk
1 red chilli (deseeded if you
    don't want it too spicy),
    finely chopped
juice of ½ lime
1 tbsp nam pla (fish sauce)
1 tsp palm sugar

Leather trousers may be last season, but you've outgrown them quite literally. Don't punish yourself by going on a diet that forces you to eat liquidised beansprouts and counts rice cakes as a major food group – just eat something healthy and delicious instead. The brown rice in this salad burns slowly, meaning you won't be plagued by the mid-afternoon munchies.

To make the dressing, whisk the coconut milk, chilli, lime juice and fish sauce together and stir in the palm sugar, mixing until it has dissolved.

Cook the rice in a large pan of salted water for about 20 minutes until it is just done. Drain and leave to cool.

Toss together the cooled rice, crayfish, cucumber, spring onions and mango and sprinkle with the coriander. Pour the dressing over the salad and mix well, then finish with a sprinkling of peanuts.

WARM BEETROOT, BEAN & FETA SALAD

The beauty of this skinny salad rests on the balance of contrasts.

There's the salty, creamy feta, the sweet and tart beetroot and the delicate, crunchy beans that make each forkful an utter delight. You'll wonder why you waited this long to go on a health kick.

Preheat the oven to 200°C/400°F/gas 6. Place the beetroot in a roasting tin, drizzle with a little of the olive oil and roast for 20–25 minutes or until cooked through.

Meanwhile, cook the runner beans in plenty of boiling salted water for 2–3 minutes. Drain and refresh in cold water to keep them crunchy, then drain again.

To assemble the salad, place the rocket and runner beans in a serving bowl, lay the warm beetroot over them and then crumble on the feta cheese. Drizzle with the remaining olive oil and the balsamic vinegar and top with the capers. Eat before the scarlet stain of the beetroot turns the salad into what looks like a crime scene.

SERVES 4

6–8 small beetroots, peeled and quartered
3 tbsp olive oil
100g/3½oz runner beans, sliced
sea salt
40g/1½oz wild rocket
150g/5oz feta cheese
2 tbsp good-quality balsamic vinegar
2 tbsp capers

HANOI POACHED CHICKEN
WITH RICE & CHILLI SAUCE

Diet food can be dull, but for all those dishes dressed with denial, there are those that are kind to your hips and packed with flavour.

SERVES 6

For the chicken and rice

1 litre/1¾ pints chicken stock
1 fat 7.5cm/3in knob of
    unpeeled fresh root ginger,
    cut into thick slices
6 spring onions, thickly
    chopped including the dark
    green parts
sea salt
6 chicken breasts, skinned
    and boned
1 tbsp sesame oil
8 fat garlic cloves, chopped
250g/9oz long-grain rice
fresh coriander leaves,
    to garnish

For the chilli sauce

2 red chillies (deseeded if
    you don't want it too spicy)
5 garlic cloves
2 tbsp light soy sauce
1 tsp caster sugar
juice of 1 lime

Poaching chicken is brilliantly healthy. Cooking it this way, in an aromatic steamy bath of stock, keeps it tasting so divine, you'll forget it's good for you! Add to that the zingy chilli sauce and garlic rice – and you'll be in food heaven!

Start off by making the chilli sauce. Put the chillies and garlic into a food processor and whiz until they are finely chopped, then mix with the remaining chilli-sauce ingredients.

To poach the chicken, bring the chicken stock to the boil and throw in the ginger and spring onions. Season with salt if necessary. Now lower the heat until you have a gentle simmer and add the chicken breasts. Cover the pan and cook for around 20–25 minutes, until the chicken is tender and cooked through.

Once the chicken is cooked you can get on with making the rice. Remove the chicken from the stock and cover it with kitchen foil to keep it warm. Strain the stock and keep it hot. In a wok, heat the sesame oil and fry the garlic until fragrant. Now add the rice and stir-fry for about 3 minutes until it's coated with the oil. Add 600ml/1 pint of the stock to the rice and cook, covered, on a low heat for about 15 minutes, until the liquid has been completely absorbed and the rice is perfectly cooked.

Whisk 200ml/7fl oz of the remaining stock into the chilli sauce.

To serve, arrange the rice and chicken on a platter and the sauce in individual dipping bowls. Scatter the rice and chicken with fresh coriander leaves.

FISH HARYALI

Eating bland food is only going to make you want to down a hefty burger and chips in one, so the trick to sticking to healthy food is to oomph up the taste factor with herbs and spices.

SERVES 4–6

½ bunch of fresh mint leaves

1 bunch of fresh coriander leaves

7.5cm/3in knob of fresh root
    ginger, peeled and roughly
    chopped

4 garlic cloves, roughly chopped

2 green chillies (deseeded if
    you don't want it too spicy),
    roughly chopped

200g/7oz yoghurt

½ tsp turmeric

juice of 1 lime

sea salt

1kg/2¼lb monkish or any other
    firm white-fleshed fish fillets,
    cut into bite-sized chunks

For the stir-fried cabbage

2 tbsp olive oil

1 tsp mustard seeds

1 pinch of asafoetida
    (see page 183)

3 green chillies (deseeded if you
    don't want it too spicy), slit

1 white cabbage, finely shredded

1 tsp caster sugar

1 pinch of turmeric

juice of 1 lemon

sea salt

The tender fish in this recipe is anointed with a luscious green herb paste (*haryali* means verdant), and served up with an exciting cabbage stir-fry you'll want to stick to your diet for.

To make the marinade, whiz together the mint leaves, coriander leaves, ginger, garlic and chillies in a food processor with a few tablespoons of water until you have a lovely emerald paste. Mix the paste into the yoghurt and then add the turmeric, lime juice and seasoning. Add the fish to the marinade and turn to coat well. Leave to marinate overnight or for at least 2 hours. Soak some wooden skewers in water at the same time.

Once you are ready to cook, preheat your grill to a medium heat. Thread the fish onto the skewers and cook under the grill for 10–12 minutes, basting with the excess marinade and turning once to cook evenly.

To make the stir-fried cabbage, begin by tempering the spices. Heat the olive oil and then sprinkle in the mustard seeds. As soon as they have popped, add the asafoetida and green chillies. Stir-fry for a few seconds, then add the cabbage and toss and stir-fry over a high heat for 3 minutes. Add the sugar, turmeric, lemon juice and salt to taste, toss and cook for another minute, then serve immediately with the fish.

LAMB KEBABS WITH TZATZIKI

I'm no glycaemic index-counting food fascist — I live for the occasional treat.

SERVES 6

600g/1lb 5oz minced lamb
grated zest of 1 lemon
½ tsp freshly ground
    nutmeg
1 tsp hot paprika
1 handful of fresh mint,
    finely chopped
2 handfuls of fresh flat-leaf
    parsley, finely chopped
1 tsp cumin seeds
1 tsp coriander seeds
¼ tsp cloves
½ tsp ground cinnamon
1 onion, roughly chopped
3 garlic cloves, roughly
    chopped
sea salt and freshly ground
    black pepper

For the tzatziki

2 Lebanese cucumbers,
    deseeded and chopped
400g/14oz natural yoghurt
1 garlic clove, crushed
juice of ½ lemon
½ tsp toasted cracked cumin
1 handful of chopped fresh
    mint

Kebabs are the kind of no-hype food that guarantee delicious, lip-smacking satisfaction, so – diet or no diet – I want to eat them. Resist the midnight booty call to the late-nite kebab joint, though, and make them at home – they'll be fresher, tastier and your waist will feel much wispier for it.

Preheat the grill to medium. Soak 12 wooden skewers in water.

Place the lamb in a mixing bowl along with the lemon zest, nutmeg, paprika, mint and parsley. Toast the cumin and coriander seeds and cloves in a dry hot pan until aromatic, then crush in a mortar and pestle to a coarse powder. Add the cinnamon and combine with the minced lamb. Put the onion and garlic into a food processor and blitz to a fine paste, then add the lamb and blitz again until you have a sticky mixture. Season with salt and pepper.

Shape the lamb mixture into 12 small kebabs around the skewers. Grill for 8–10 minutes, turning frequently, until they are cooked through.

To make the tzatziki, mix all the ingredients in a bowl with seasoning to taste until you have a thick yoghurt dip. Serve with the kebabs.

MISO-GLAZED TUNA
WITH SHIITAKE MUSHROOM BROTH

Using a marinade is a good way of adding flavour without piling on the calories, and the magic of miso speeds up your metabolism.

To make the marinade, whisk the miso paste into all the liquid ingredients. Add the ginger and sugar, stir to mix and dissolve the sugar, then pour it over the tuna, making sure the fish is coated well on both sides. Cover and marinate for about 1 hour.

Now for the mushroom broth. Whisk the miso paste with the water, bring it to the boil, then lower the heat to a gentle simmer. Add the noodles, ginger and mushrooms and simmer until the noodles are just cooked – 4–5 minutes. Finally, stir in the pak choi, spring onions and soy sauce. Cook briefly and then garnish with the coriander.

To cook the tuna, heat a griddle or frying pan until very hot, then brush the excess marinade off the fish and place in the pan. Cook for about 2 minutes on each side, so that it is seared on the outside but still rare on the inside.

To serve, place a bed of noodles in the centre of a bowl, pour the mushroom broth over them and then place the tuna on top. Dress with the spring onions.

SERVES 4

4 × 225g/8oz tuna fillets
chopped spring onions,
   to garnish

For the miso marinade

6 tbsp white miso paste
4 tbsp mirin
2 tbsp rice vinegar
1 tbsp freshly grated root
   ginger
2 tbsp brown sugar

For the mushroom broth

4 tbsp white miso paste
1.5 litres/2½ pints hot water
100g/3½oz soba noodles
1 tsp freshly grated root
   ginger
1 handful of sliced shiitake
   mushrooms
1 handful of torn pak choi
3 spring onions, finely sliced
2 tbsp light soy sauce
3 tbsp chopped fresh
   coriander

INDIAN FISHCAKES

These fishcakes are far removed from the usual tasteless diet offerings.

MAKES 30 SMALL FISHCAKES

5 fat garlic cloves, roughly chopped
2 red chillies (deseeded if you don't want it too spicy), roughly chopped
7.5cm/3in knob of fresh root ginger, peeled and roughly chopped
800g/1¾lb pollack or cod, skinned and pinboned
2 tbsp fennel seeds
1 tbsp toasted cumin seeds
1 tbsp carom seeds
1 tsp sea salt
1 tsp coarsely ground black pepper
zest and juice of 1 lime
100g/3½oz green beans, finely chopped
1 large handful of fresh coriander, chopped
1 egg to bind
3 tbsp gram flour
olive oil for frying
coriander chutney, to serve

With tender chunks of white fish and juicy green beans, all spiced up with the usual suspects from the Indian spice cupboard, they're a total treat.

Put the garlic, chillies and ginger into a food processor and blitz to a fine paste. Next, add the fish to the blender and blitz until it is finely chopped. Transfer the fish and spice paste to a mixing bowl and mix with the fennel, cumin and carom seeds, salt and pepper. Stir in the lime zest, green beans and coriander and squeeze in the lime juice. Stir to combine all the ingredients and mix in the beaten egg and gram flour to bind, then shape tablespoons of the mixture into small flat patties.

Heat a little olive oil in a frying pan over a medium heat and fry the fishcakes for 3 minutes on each side until golden and cooked through. Serve with coriander chutney.

KITCHEN-ADE
To get a dose of healthy fish oils, use half cod and half salmon fillets.

CHAPTER TEN

Food rehab

No need to go cold turkey

New Year's Resolutions

1999 – Get Richer, Lose Weight.

2000 – Get Spiritual, Lose Weight.

2005 – Find 'The One', Lose Weight.

2009 – Darn...

...you get the picture! Weigh-ins after holidays are enough to depress even the skinniest of minnies, so before you even think of pulling on your Spanx and dusting down another tasteless rice cake, check into my food rehab clinic. Here, the word 'detox' is banned and denial is just for dummies.

Think of food as a prescription. It will give you energy, wellbeing and, well... glossier hair! Warming lamb stew and pomegranate-glazed pork – not such a bitter pill to swallow.

LAMB STEW WITH TURNIPS, PEARL BARLEY & A GARLIC BREAD CRUST

There's nothing like a good power stew to perk up the tired and dreary.

SERVES 6

1 tbsp olive oil

500g/1lb 2oz diced boneless lamb shoulder

2 tbsp plain flour

1 knob of unsalted butter

3 celery sticks, chopped into large chunks

1 leek, trimmed and chopped into thick rounds

300g/10oz small turnips, quartered

½ tsp chilli flakes

2 bay leaves

2 sprigs of rosemary

100g/3½oz pearl barley

500ml/18fl oz hot chicken or lamb stock

sea salt and freshly ground black pepper

For the crust

1 medium French baguette

3 garlic cloves, chopped

½ tsp sea salt

1 tbsp chopped fresh flat-leaf parsley

25g/1oz soft unsalted butter

This one is packed with pearl barley, which is rich in fibre, vitamins and minerals and barely contains a trace of fat. The best thing about this stew is that once you've got it all in the pan, you can leave it on the hob and forget about it for an hour or so, giving you plenty of time to go and have that all-important power snooze.

Heat the olive oil in a casserole. Dust the chunks of lamb with the flour, dust off any excess flour and then brown the lamb in the casserole on all sides. Remove from the pan with a slotted spoon and leave to rest on a plate.

Melt the butter in the same pan. Sauté the celery, leek and turnips for 10–15 minutes until they have caught some colour and caramelised slightly. Return the sealed lamb to the pan, add the chilli flakes, bay leaves and rosemary and fry again for 1 minute. Pour in the pearl barley and hot stock and season well. Cover and leave to simmer on a low heat for 1 hour, topping it up with water if needed.

Preheat the oven to 200°C/400°F/gas 6. Cut the French baguette into slices on the diagonal. Make the garlic butter by pounding together the garlic, salt and parsley, then stir in the softened butter. Butter one side of each slice. Take the casserole off the heat and arrange the sliced bread over the surface. Bake it in the oven for 20 minutes or until the bread is golden and crisp. Serve piping hot.

MUNG BEAN & BROWN RICE KEDGEREE

Kedgeree is the anglicised term for 'khichdee', a simple dish of lentils and rice that's been eaten all over India for centuries.

SERVES 6

4 tbsp vegetable oil
1 onion, sliced
1 tsp sea salt
7.5cm/3in knob of fresh root
    ginger, peeled and finely
    chopped
5 garlic cloves, finely sliced
2 tsp coarsely crushed black
    peppercorns
300g/10oz mung beans
1 litre/1¾ pints water

For the rice
300ml/10fl oz boiling water
150g/5oz brown basmati rice

To serve
6 hard-boiled eggs,
    quartered
natural yoghurt
hot lime pickle

The addition of smoked fish only came with India's colonisation. This is my un-anglicised recipe, where the brown rice and mung beans combine to give the perfect balance of carbs and protein, and with the addition of mood-boosting ginger it's virtually Prozac on a plate.

Heat the vegetable oil in a heavy-based saucepan and fry the onion with the salt to stop it catching – you want beautifully soft melt-in-the-mouth onion here. Stir in the ginger, garlic and black pepper and fry again over a medium heat for 2 minutes. Stir in the mung beans, along with the cold water. Bring to the boil, then turn the heat to low, cover the pan and let the beans simmer for about 30 minutes until they are tender. Test a grain – if it mushes easily, you're ready to add the rice.

Pour the boiling water and rice into the mung bean mixture, cover the pan and cook for about 20 minutes until all the water has been absorbed.

To serve, top each portion with a hard-boiled egg and accompany with natural yoghurt and hot lime pickle.

SOY & GINGER CRISPY-SKIN SALMON

Salmon is hailed for being heart-healthy, as it's packed with omega-3 fatty acids.

This recipe is good for your heart in more than one way, though – it's so quick and easy to do, it means you'll have time for that quick visit to the gym after all! I enjoy it with some steamed greens and rice or on a bed of noodles.

There are a few rules to getting deliciously crisp skin on fish. First, make sure the fish is scaled. If your fishmonger hasn't done it, it really is a doddle, so don't fret. Hold the fish over the sink and scrape a spoon against the grain of the skin and you should see the scales flying off.

The second rule is that the skin should be dry, so pat off any moisture with kitchen paper. Pat a layer of sea salt on the skin of the fish and leave for 10 minutes. This will help draw out any excess moisture held in the skin. Scrape off the salt and then get the ingredients for the marinade ready.

Mix the ingredients for the marinade in a bowl and then add the salmon flesh-side down making sure the skin does not get wet. Cover and leave for at least 20 minutes.

Pour a little olive oil in a frying pan, enough to coat the bottom of the pan, and heat over a medium heat. When it is hot, place the fish, skin-side down, into the pan, pushing the skin down so it gets crisp and golden. After 3 minutes or so, flip the fish over to the fleshy side and cook again. This should take roughly 3–4 minutes depending on the thickness of the fish, but you'll know it's cooked when it turns opaque. Serve with steamed greens and rice or on a bed of noodles.

SERVES 4

4 salmon fillets, skin on
sea salt
olive oil for frying
steamed greens and rice or
   noodles, to serve

For the marinade

4 tbsp freshly chopped
   root ginger
3 tbsp runny honey
2 tbsp olive oil
1 red chilli (deseeded if you
   don't want it too spicy),
   finely sliced
juice of 1 lime
4 tbsp light soy sauce

ROSEMARY & CHILLI SALT ALMONDS

Things to do today: pay phone bill. Insure car. Full leg and bikini wax. Meet work deadline. Phew!

SERVES 6–8

1 tbsp sea salt
1½ tbsp chopped fresh
   rosemary leaves
½ tsp chilli flakes
20g/¾oz unsalted butter
300g/10oz almonds

If you're a busy bee, you need proper sustenance and a line of Red Bulls just isn't going to cut it. My mother swears that munching 12 almonds a day boosts your energy. Well, who am I to argue – mother knows best!

Preheat the oven to 190°C/375°F/gas 5. Put the salt, rosemary and chilli flakes into a pestle and mortar and bash a few times to bruise the rosemary.

Melt the butter on a baking sheet or roasting tin and toss the almonds through it, making sure they are all well coated with butter. Sprinkle on the rosemary chilli salt and toss again, then transfer to the oven and bake for 15–20 minutes. These will keep in an airtight jar for 7–10 days.

GRILLED LEMON & THYME MACKEREL

WITH MUSTARD & GREEN BEAN SALAD

Want shiny hair and glowing skin? Well, who doesn't?

SERVES 4

4 whole mackerel,
    each weighing
    400–500g/14oz–1lb 2oz,
    gutted
1 lemon, finely sliced
6 sprigs of thyme
2 tbsp olive oil
sea salt and freshly ground
    black pepper

For the potato salad
500g/1lb 2oz new potatoes,
    scrubbed
300g/10oz green beans
1 generous handful of
    chopped fresh flat-leaf
    parsley

For the mustard dressing
6 tbsp olive oil
2 tbsp wholegrain mustard
1 tbsp white wine vinegar
1 tsp caster sugar

Before you re-mortgage your house to splurge on the latest buzz skincare, though, try mackerel for dinner. Now, here's the science bit: mackerel, like salmon, is full of omega-3 fatty acids, which are known to prevent heart disease, ease creaking joints and fight depression. Above all, it gives you lustrous locks and enviable skin. Second helpings? I thought so.

First, make the potato salad. Simmer the potatoes in boiling water until just tender. Meanwhile, blanch the green beans in boiling water for 2 minutes, drain and refresh in cold water to maintain their crispness, then drain again. For the mustard dressing, whisk together the olive oil, mustard, vinegar and sugar with salt and pepper to taste. Drain the potatoes and combine with the beans. While the potatoes are still warm, pour the dressing over them – they absorb more of the dressing when they are warm. Add the chopped parsley and toss to coat.

Preheat a grill to medium heat. Make several slits on one side of each mackerel, making sure you do not cut through the bone. Season the fish inside and out, then stuff each cavity with the lemon slices, and the slits with the sprigs of thyme. Drizzle a little olive oil over the fish and cook under the grill for 5 minutes on each side until the flesh is opaque.

Eat immediately with a generous helping of potato salad.

ORECCHIETTE WITH CURLY KALE, LEMON & BASIL PESTO

All hail curly kale. Think of it as the new spinach.

It contains more calcium than yoghurt or spinach, and more vitamin A than cooked broccoli. Just 100g of this superleaf also has more than half your daily recommended dose of vitamin C. Cooked like this in a creamy pesto, it loses its sulphurous taste and becomes sweet and mellow. Yet another reason to go green.

Cook the pasta in boiling salted water until it's al dente. Drain.

Heat the olive oil in a pan and sauté the garlic and lemon zest for 1 minute. Toss in the kale and sauté until it has wilted – this takes just 2–3 minutes.

Next, blitz the pine nuts to a paste in a food processor, then add the double cream, lemon juice and nutmeg and blitz again. Add the basil and kale and blend again. Finally, pour in the extra virgin olive oil and whiz until you have a thick, smooth pesto. Pour into a bowl, season to taste and stir in the cheese. Pour the sauce over the cooked pasta and toss well, making sure the pasta gets a generous coating.

SERVES 4

400g/14oz orecchiette
 or penne
1 tbsp olive oil
2 garlic cloves, crushed
zest of 1 lemon
100g/3½oz curly kale,
 roughly chopped
60g/2¼oz toasted pine
 nuts
3 tbsp double cream
juice of ½ lemon
½ tsp nutmeg
1 generous handful of fresh
 basil leaves
4 tbsp extra virgin olive oil
50g/2oz freshly grated
 Parmesan cheese
sea salt and freshly ground
 black pepper

GREEN TEA NOODLE SUPERFOOD SALAD

Those seed-and-sprout munching yoga bunnies age terribly well.

SERVES 6

200g/7oz green tea noodles
    (see Kitchen-ade)
100g/3½oz green beans
100g/3½oz Tenderstem
    sprouting broccoli
1 generous handful of
    beansprouts
2 small carrots, cut into
    matchsticks
1 red and 1 yellow pepper,
    each deseeded and cut into
    thin strips
100g/3½oz trimmed asparagus
olive oil for brushing
3 tbsp mixed seeds, such as
    sunflower, pumpkin, sesame,
    linseed and hemp, to serve

For the dressing

1 garlic clove, crushed
1cm/½in knob of fresh root
    ginger, peeled and grated
1 shallot, finely chopped
4 tbsp olive oil
1 tbsp honey
3 tbsp light soy sauce
1 tsp sesame oil
1 tbsp rice vinegar
juice of ½ lime

Get in on their youthful action with this tasty salad. It's brimming with vitamins and antioxidants known for their anti-ageing benefits, and isn't half as exhausting to make as holding the downward dog. It's wrinkle-free skin on a plate – no Botox jab required.

Boil the noodles in a large pan of simmering water until cooked through. Drain and refresh in cold water, then drain again.

Steam the green beans and broccoli for 3–4 minutes, then place in a large salad bowl with the beansprouts, carrots and pepper strips. Add the drained noodles.

Heat a griddle pan until hot. Brush the asparagus with olive oil and griddle until tiger-striped and tender. Mix into the noodles.

To make the dressing, whisk all the ingredients together. Pour over the salad and toss through, then top with the mixed seeds and serve.

KITCHEN-ADE
Green tea noodles are available online at www.mountfuji.co.uk, but if you can't get hold of them, use ordinary soba noodles and put two green tea bags in the boiling water instead.

BUTTERNUT SQUASH, FETA, SEEDS & GREENS SALAD

If you're watching your waistline, you'll be delighted to know that these sweet orange squashes contain so few calories they are barely worth counting.

Added to this, they contain vitamins C and E and beta-carotene, which strengthens immunity, improves eyesight and reduces cholesterol. What's not to love?

Preheat the oven to 200°C/400°F/gas 6. Sprinkle the squash with the fennel seeds and chilli flakes and then drizzle with the olive oil, making sure that all the pieces of squash are well coated. Roast in the oven for 30 minutes or until the squash is tender.

Meanwhile, toast the seeds and pine nuts in a hot dry pan until golden, then set aside.

Lay out a bed of greens on a serving dish and tumble the squash over, making sure you don't waste a drop of the oily juices. Crumble on the feta cheese and sprinkle with the toasted seeds. Finally, drizzle with some extra virgin olive oil and balsamic vinegar.

KITCHEN-ADE

The skin of the butternut squash softens and goes chewy when cooked, so there's absolutely no need to peel it.

Reserve the seeds too, as they contain minerals and essential fats. For a healthy snack, I simply heat a pan, brush it with a little olive oil and gently toast the seeds. Finish with a tiny sprinkle of salt.

SERVES 6

1 medium butternut squash, chopped into large chunks
1 tsp fennel seeds
½ tsp chilli flakes
2 tbsp olive oil
1 tbsp sunflower seeds
1 tbsp pumpkin seeds
1 tbsp pine nuts
200g/7oz mixed greens, such as baby leaf spinach, rocket and watercress
150g/5oz feta cheese, crumbled

For the dressing
a drizzle of extra virgin olive oil
a good drizzle of aged balsamic vinegar

SOYA BEAN & TOMATO BRUSCHETTA WITH PECORINO

Haricot beans. Butter beans. Broad beans. Bean there, done that.

SERVES 6

300g/10oz frozen soya beans

300g/10oz cherry tomatoes, halved

1 handful of fresh mint, finely chopped

1 handful of fresh flat-leaf parsley, finely chopped

juice of 1 lemon

2 garlic cloves

sea salt and freshly ground black pepper

1 day-old ciabatta loaf

olive oil, to drizzle

150g/5oz pecorino cheese shavings

3 tbsp extra virgin olive oil

My latest leguminous love affair is with the soya bean. They're mainly sold frozen and, like peas, they're none the worse for it. They're as rich in protein as meat and eggs and contain a hefty dose of vitamin C too, giving them serious superfood credentials. Served on bruschetta like this, they're sweet, juicy and tender. Paired with a creamy pecorino they're magic.

Blanch the soya beans in boiling water for 2 minutes. Drain and refresh in cold water, then drain again. Mash them slightly and then combine them with the cherry tomatoes, herbs, lemon juice, garlic and seasoning. Mix well.

Heat a griddle pan until very hot. Slice the ciabatta into thick slices. Drizzle both sides of each slice with a little olive oil and griddle until golden and crisp. Transfer to a serving plate. Spoon the bean mixture over the ciabatta slices, top with the pecorino shavings and then drizzle with a little extra virgin olive oil.

POMEGRANATE-GLAZED PORK

Pomegranates are the jewels in the crown of the superfood list.

SERVES 6

olive oil for greasing and drizzling
1 boneless pork loin weighing
    about 1kg/2¼lb
4 garlic cloves, finely chopped
1 long red chilli (deseeded if you
    don't want it too spicy), finely
    chopped
sea salt and freshly ground
    black pepper

For the glaze
5 tbsp pomegranate molasses
1 tbsp ground cinnamon
1 tbsp ground coriander seeds
1 tbsp honey
1 tbsp black pepper
1 tbsp paprika

They're packed with iron and have more antioxidant properties than green tea – plus they're truly delicious. They've been enjoyed in the Middle East for years, but the West has only just caught on. Head to a Middle Eastern store and pick yourself up a bottle of pomegranate molasses – also known as grenadine molasses. It's a rich, treacly, sweet and tart syrup made from boiled-down pomegranate juice, sugar and lemon and is wonderful as a glaze, as it is here, or as a salad dressing.

Turn the oven up to its highest setting – about 240°C/475°F/gas 9. Lightly oil a roasting tin. Using a sharp knife, score the skin of the pork in a criss-cross pattern. Turn the pork over and rub the garlic, chilli and olive oil all over the flesh, but not on the skin. Turn the joint over again and pat the skin dry with kitchen paper. Once dry, generously season with salt and pepper and drizzle with some olive oil. Place the loin in the roasting tin, skin-side up, and roast in the oven for 15–20 minutes or until the skin has become pale golden. Popping it into the oven at this inferno temperature is what makes the crackling irresistibly crispy.

Meanwhile, whisk together all the ingredients for the glaze and put to one side.

Once your crackling has some colour, remove the pork from the oven and turn the temperature down to 180°C/350°F/gas 4. Generously brush the top and sides of the meat with one-third of the glaze. Put it back into the oven for about 20 minutes and then baste again. Do this three times in total. You should cook your pork for about 25 minutes for every 450g/1lb it weighs, so a 1kg/2¼lb joint should take about 1 hour.

Rest the meat for about 15 minutes. Carve and then spoon some of the pan juices over it to serve.

GOJI BERRY & NUT FLAPJACKS

Have a nibble — they're berry good for you.

I'm a sucker for miracle cures, so when I heard about the cellulite-banishing, anti-ageing, natural aphrodisiac and cheering properties of these little shrivelled garnet berries I had to make a flapjack out of them.

Preheat the oven to 180°C/350°F/gas 4. Line a baking sheet with baking parchment.

Melt the butter, sugar and golden syrup in a large saucepan over a low heat and keep stirring until the sugar has dissolved. Stir in the berries, nuts and jumbo oats, then pour into the tray, pressing the mixture down firmly so that you have an even surface.

Bake in the oven for 25 minutes and then leave to cool. Once cooled, cut into thick slices.

MAKES 10 SLICES

125g/4oz unsalted butter

50g/2oz golden caster sugar

4 tbsp golden syrup

45g/1¾oz goji berries

45g/1¾oz toasted flaked almonds

45g/1¾oz toasted hazelnuts, halved

250g/9oz jumbo oats

CHAPTER ELEVEN

Fork me, spoon me

The food of love and rude food

Good food is all about good partnerships – fish and chips, pie and mash, strawberries and cream – but nothing partners better with a hot dish than good loving ... mmmmm.

It may be my imagination, dear reader – and it does run wild at the best of times – but there's something about feeding a lover that makes them putty in your hands. Everything is just so negotiable over a dreamy dessert and bedroom eyes. In other words, use the exceedingly tasty morsel on his plate as bedroom currency – you'll be surprised at what a perfectly done scallop will buy!

So here's to ditching those 'be seen there' chi-chi restaurants in favour of your front room. Put on your best lingerie, dust down that pinny and have a culinary night in – at least that way you won't have far to go when things get cookin' outside of the kitchen.

SCALLOPS WITH CHAMPAGNE BUTTER SAUCE

This silky, sexy champagne sauce is the icing on the cake for a well-turned-out scallop.

SERVES 2

8 plump scallops, washed
    and trimmed
sea salt and freshly ground
    black pepper
lemon wedges, to serve

**For the champagne
butter sauce**

2 tbsp finely chopped shallots
    or red onion
1 tbsp olive oil
100ml/3½fl oz champagne
½ tsp black peppercorns
1 bay leaf
85g/3¼oz cold unsalted
    butter, chopped into cubes,
    plus 1 knob
1 heaped tbsp chopped fresh
    flat-leaf parsley

What's more, once you have popped the cork of a large bottle of bubbly and used a little for the sauce, you can but only quaff the rest – well, it would be a shame not to! Bottoms up!

Begin by seasoning your scallops generously on both sides with plenty of salt and pepper.

To make the champagne butter sauce, fry the onions in the olive oil, then pour the champagne into the pan. Add the peppercorns and bay leaf to the boozy liquid, increase the heat and cook until the liquid is reduced by half, then strain into a heatproof bowl. Place the champagne reduction over a double boiler on a low heat and whisk in the butter, a little at a time, until you have a gloriously satin sauce. Stir in the parsley and keep the sauce warm while you pan-fry the scallops.

Heat the knob of butter in a large frying pan. When it is hot, add the scallops, making sure you don't overcrowd the pan. The scallops should sizzle on contact with the hot butter. Fry for 2 minutes on each side until the skin goes golden and a little crusty. Serve straight away with a drizzle of the sauce and a wedge of lemon

OOZING GOAT'S CHEESE IN TOMATO SAUCE

Romance can come with a variety of cheesy gestures, from cutesy pet names to matching outfits.

So, given our love of *le fromage*, here's another to add to the list. The only difference being, this is unlikely to turn anyone's stomach.

Roasting the tomatoes like this means you intensify their flavour to the max – so even if you don't have the best ones to hand, you'll still turn out a sauce that packs a punch. I especially love the way the cheese gets a handsome golden crust on top and oozes seductively into the sauce underneath. Serve up with crusty bread for desire on a dinner plate.

Preheat the oven to 190°C/375°F/gas 5. Spread the tomatoes out in a roasting tin and sprinkle with the garlic, balsamic, honey, chilli, olive oil, thyme and salt and pepper. Roast for 35 minutes until the tomatoes have blistered and softened. Put into a blender along with the sun-dried tomato paste and blitz until you have a rich tomato sauce.

Divide the sauce between two 250ml/8fl oz ramekins and place a slice of goat's cheese on top of each. Place a basil leaf on the cheese and drizzle with extra virgin olive oil. Bake for 15 minutes until the cheese is oven-singed and oozing. Serve with hunks of crusty bread to dip into it.

SERVES 2

300g/10oz ripe tomatoes, quartered
3 garlic cloves, sliced
1 tbsp balsamic vinegar
2 tbsp honey
1 tsp dried chilli flakes
2 tbsp olive oil
leaves stripped from 6 sprigs of fresh thyme
sea salt and freshly ground black pepper
1 tbsp sun-dried tomato paste
100g/3½oz soft goat's cheese, cut into 2 slices
2 fresh basil leaves
extra virgin olive oil, to drizzle

GRILLED OYSTERS WITH GARLIC & PARSLEY BREADCRUMBS

Most chefs think cooking an oyster is like gilding a lily, a sacrilegious act, but I guarantee these are delightful and still do the job – wink wink!

Eating oysters for me used to be a show of sexual prowess – that is until I was poisoned by one that wasn't so fresh. It was a hot night with an even hotter date, and I was seductively downing my sixth mood-boosting mollusc of the night, when all of a sudden I felt rather peculiar! The date came to an emergency end and needless to say I never heard from him again.

Since then, I've only been able to stomach these aphrodisiac delicacies if they're cooked.

Begin by steaming the oysters for about 2 minutes until they peek open. Meanwhile, make the garlic parsley butter. Mash together the parsley, garlic and butter, season well and add the breadcrumbs. Preheat the grill to medium heat.

Fill a roasting tin with rock salt – this will not only make an attractive base for your oysters, it will also help support them. Open up each oyster and cut out from the shell. Take care not to lose any of the juices. Place the oyster meat and juice in the deeper shell and top with the breadcrumb mix. Arrange on the salt base and then grill for about 2 minutes until they're golden brown and bubbling. Down in one.

SERVES 2

6 oysters in their shells
1 tbsp chopped fresh flat-leaf parsley
2 garlic cloves, finely chopped
30g/generous 1oz unsalted butter, softened
sea salt and freshly ground black pepper
2 tbsp toasted brown breadcrumbs
rock salt

KITCHEN-ADE

Rock oysters are best to use for this recipe as they aren't as expensive as native oysters and have deeper shells. The flatter native oysters are expensive and best eaten as they come.

GRIDDLED BALSAMIC ASPARAGUS & PARMA HAM KISSES

I call these wraps of asparagus kisses, because when they are bound with the ham they look like an 'x' at the foot of a love letter.

SERVES 2

½ tsp caster sugar
1 tbsp balsamic vinegar
2 tbsp olive oil
dried chilli flakes (optional)
12 fine spears of asparagus,
   the woody stems
   snapped off
6 slices of Parma ham

Wrap the silky ham around the asparagus as tightly as a lover's possessive embrace and griddle until caramelised and singed. Eating these with your fingers makes them even tastier.

In a flat dish, whisk the sugar, balsamic vinegar and olive oil until you have a glossy emulsion. For those who like it hot, I suggest adding a few flame flecks of dried red chilli. Take two spears of asparagus and cross them over so they look like a kiss. Wrap one slice of Parma ham through the middle of the spears to secure tightly. Repeat with the remaining asparagus and Parma ham to make six bundles.

Heat a pan until it's medium hot. Dip each bundle in the oily vinegar, making sure the spears are well anointed, and then cook them for 2 minutes on each side until the ham has crisped up and the asparagus is tender but still has bite. Be careful not to overcrowd the pan here, or you will end up with disappointingly soggy asparagus. Serve pronto.

KITCHEN-ADE

If your asparagus is quite thick, blanch in boiling water for 2 minutes before wrapping with ham and griddling.

LOVE APPLE & FETA TARTS

It isn't surprising to me that our ancestors once called tomatoes love apples.

If you have ever tried biting into a buxom, well-ripened tomato in the middle of summer, the juice running down your chin, you'll completely appreciate that it is erotic eating at its very best. The saltiness of the feta works really well with the sweet tomatoes here, and, of course, the unnecessary but indulgent heart-shaped pastry is bound to make your sweetheart feel cherished.

Preheat the oven to 220°C/425°F/gas 7. Roll out the pastry on a lightly floured surface until it is 5mm/¼in thick. Next, use a 12cm/5in heart-shaped pastry cutter to cut out two shapes from the pastry. If you don't have a cutter, make yourself a paper template, place on the pastry and cut around it with a sharp knife.

Score a line on the pastry about 1cm/½in in from the edge – this will create a proud, heightened crust. Using a fork, prick the base of the pastry all over, except the crust. Sprinkle over half the feta cheese and then layer on the juicy tomatoes. Top with the rest of the feta and the thyme, then drizzle with extra virgin olive oil and season.

Brush the edges of the pastry with the beaten egg to get a golden glaze, then bake for 20 minutes until the pastry is flakily crackly and cooked through.

Serve with some torn basil, a drizzle of extra virgin olive oil and a touch of balsamic vinegar.

SERVES 2

plain flour, to dust
200g/7oz ready-made
    puff pastry
100g/3½oz feta cheese
12 cherry tomatoes, halved
4 sprigs of thyme
extra virgin olive oil,
    to drizzle
sea salt and freshly ground
    black pepper
1 egg, beaten
1 tbsp torn fresh basil leaves
aged balsamic vinegar,
    to drizzle

KITCHEN-ADE

If you don't want to go to the fuss of heart-shaped pastry, just roll out your pastry and cut it into two oblongs.

A few chopped kalamata olives are also a tasty addition to the topping.

SEXY RACK OF RAS AL HANOUT LAMB WITH POTATO & SAFFRON RICE

These sexy racks hold all the seductive exoticism of a whole 1001 Arabian nights.

SERVES 2

2 fat garlic cloves, crushed
1 tsp sea salt
zest and juice of 1 lemon
5 tbsp olive oil
3 tbsp ras al hanout (see
    page 242) or from a tin
2 trimmed racks of lamb
fresh mint leaves to serve

For the potato-crusted saffron rice

6 baby new potatoes
125g/4oz basmati rice
1 large pinch of saffron
    strands soaked in 1 tbsp
    warm water
1 knob of unsalted butter
olive oil, to grease
sea salt

In Morocco *Ras al hanout* quite literally translates as 'top of the shelf' – meaning a blend of the vendor's premium spices. There is something about crushing your own blend that is extra sexy – the aroma, and a little bit of labour, creates an erotic anticipation. With its heady musk of aphrodisiac rose petals and warm heat of cinnamon, this spice-crusted lamb is a sure way to ensure some top-shelf action of your very own...

Stir the garlic, salt, lemon zest and juice and olive oil into the ras al hanout to make a lavish paste. Score the fat on the lamb racks lightly and then smear on the paste. Leave to marinate for at least 2 hours or overnight, so that the redolent spices really cut through the fat and perfume the meat.

An hour before you are ready to cook the lamb, prepare the rice. Preheat the oven to 220°C/425°F/gas 7. Parboil the potatoes, drain and then cut into thin slices. Boil the rice in plenty of simmering salted water for 6–8 minutes until the grains are half cooked. Drain, then spread over a plate and sprinkle with half the saffron and liquid. In a pan, heat the butter over a gentle flame until it is molten, then add the remaining saffron. Tumble in the potatoes and toss to coat until they are all tinted with the lovely golden butter.

Grease two ramekins with a little olive oil and line their bases with the saffron potatoes. Top with the half-cooked rice, making sure you pack it in tightly. Pour the leftover saffron butter onto the rice, then cover the tops of the ramekins with kitchen foil and cook in the oven for 25 minutes on the bottom shelf.

To cook the lamb, heat a pan until very hot, then fry the racks on all sides for 2 minutes – getting a colour on them at this stage means you will get lots more flavour. Transfer them to a roasting tin and cook in the oven for 10 minutes if you want them rare and 15–20 minutes for medium to well done. Cover the meat with kitchen foil and let it rest for 10 minutes before slicing.

Invert the rice onto two plates and serve with the sliced lamb racks and a little fresh mint on the side.

RAS AL HANOUT

seeds from 3 green
    cardamom pods
½ tsp cloves
1 tsp coriander seeds
1 tsp cumin seeds
1 tsp fennel seeds
1 star anise
1 small blade of mace
½ tsp sweet paprika
½ tsp turmeric
1 tsp ground cinnamon
a generous pinch of
    saffron strands
1 tbsp dried Damascan
    rose petals
a good grating of fresh
    nutmeg

To make your own ras al hanout, heat a pan until very hot. Dry-roast the whole spices until they release their intoxicating fragrance and start to pop. Work fast to make sure that you don't burn them. Transfer them into a mortar, add all the ready-ground spices and remaining ingredients and then bash with the pestle until you have a coarse powder.

PROSECCO RISOTTO WITH ASPARAGUS

I sometimes like to eat risotto as an accompaniment to roasted scallops or a fillet of fish, but this one, even without the addition of the asparagus, is majestic enough to stand tastily alone.

If you're feeling flush, or in the unlikely event you have any left over, you can use champagne, but I find a decent bottle of Prosecco does the job just fine. As a plate of food, this one is no doubt simple and comforting, but there is also a subtle sexiness to it. When the cold butter is beaten in at the end, it transforms the risotto into a sheeny pool of molten deliciousness. Serve and seduce.

Heat the stock in a pan and keep on a low simmer. If you are entertaining a vegetarian, by all means use a vegetable stock, but I find chicken stock tends to give this dish a densely savoury flavour and a gorgeous sunlit glaze.

Heat a griddle or frying pan until very hot. Brush the asparagus with 1 tablespoon of the olive oil and griddle or pan fry until it is tender and tiger-striped. Remove from the pan and set aside.

In a heavy-based pan, heat the remaining olive oil and the melt the butter. Sauté the onion and lemon zest until softened but still pale. Next, stir in the rice, coating it well with the molten butter, and cook for a while until it starts to turn translucent at the edges. Pour in the Prosecco and let it bubble and boil until all the alcohol has evaporated. Pour in the stock, a ladleful at a time, stirring until all the liquid has been absorbed before adding the next amount. Once all the liquid has been absorbed, beat in the cold butter and Parmesan cheese. Stir through the asparagus and scatter with the parsley. Don't waste any time in serving this up, or indeed gobbling it up.

SERVES 2

500ml/18fl oz chicken or vegetable stock
100g/3½oz asparagus, trimmed
2 tbsp olive oil
25g/1oz unsalted butter, plus 50g/2oz cold unsalted butter to add in at the end
1 small onion, chopped
zest of ½ lemon
200g/7oz arborio rice
150ml/5fl oz Prosecco
30g/generous 1oz Parmesan cheese
3 tbsp chopped fresh flat-leaf parsley
sea salt and freshly ground black pepper

KITCHEN-ADE

For perfectly creamy risotto with bite, use a wooden spoon to stir it in one direction only. Stirring it both ways breaks down the grains of rice.

SAFFRON FISH STEW

Saffron is one of the most ancient and expensive spices. It takes a harvest of 70,000 crocuses to get just one pound of saffron!

SERVES 2

a generous glug of olive oil
1 red onion, thickly sliced
1 small fennel bulb, cut into
    chunky slices
3 garlic cloves
1 bay leaf
1 red chilli (deseeded if you don't
    want it too spicy), thickly sliced
1 tsp fennel seeds
250ml/8fl oz white wine
600ml/1 pint hot fish stock
500g/1lb 2oz ripe tomatoes,
    chopped
1 large pinch of saffron strands,
    pounded in a little warm water
200g/7oz any firm white-fleshed
    fish, cut into bite-sized chunks
    (I tend to use monkfish)
6–8 mussels
200g/7oz baby squid, cleaned
    (see page 134) and cut into rings
6 unpeeled fresh langoustines
    or 8 raw tiger prawns
150g/5oz peas
1 tsp chopped fennel fronds
1 tbsp chopped fresh flat-leaf
    parsley
sea salt and freshly ground black
    pepper

Thankfully, knocking up this stew is nowhere near as labour intensive. I love how the milky white fish takes on the saffron's beautiful ochre stain and delicate flavour. Serving a lover a plateful of this is bound to make him think you're a catch.

Heat the olive oil in a large pan and then fry the onion and fennel until softened and just beginning to catch on the bottom of the pan. Add the whole, peeled garlic cloves and bay leaf and then the chilli and fennel seeds. (I leave the garlic whole here because I want a gentle background flavour rather than a full-on fierce kiss.) Cook for another 3 minutes, then splash in the wine to deglaze the pan. Scrape off all the bits caught on the bottom of the pan and cook until the wine is reduced by half. Pour in the hot stock and add the tomatoes and saffron. Cover and cook on a low heat for about 10 minutes.

Once the stew has thickened a little, add the fish and cook for 5 minutes. Then add the mussels, squid and langoustines or prawns and peas, cover the pan and cook for 3–4 minutes, until the shellfish are pink through and the mussels have opened up. Fish out and discard any mussels that haven't opened. Scatter the fennel fronds and parsley over the stew and serve with fresh bread.

KITCHEN-ADE
I sometimes add potatoes to the stew, but you can pretty much try it with any vegetables you like.

ROASTED PAPRIKA QUAILS WITH ROMESCO SAUCE

This miniscule bird demands the downing of forks and knives in favour of fingers.

Tearing away at the succulent flesh dipped in vermillion sauce, the delicate bones gnawed to snapping point, is a hedonistic, ice-breaking pleasure. A plate clean apart from a pile of skinny broken bones will be proof enough that your guest is having a 'quail' of a time!

Combine the paprika, olive oil and thyme with salt and pepper to taste and then rub all over the quails, making sure you get under the skin too. Leave them to marinate for an hour or so, or overnight is fine if you want to start your preparation a day early.

When you are ready to roast them, preheat the oven to 190°C/375°F/gas 5. Place the quails on a wire rack over a roasting tin and roast for 25 minutes or so, or until the skin is more-ishly crispy and charred and the juices run clear when you pierce the bird with a knife.

While the quails are roasting, make the romesco sauce. Simply combine the almonds and bread in a food processor and blitz to a crumble. Add the tomatoes, sliced peppers, garlic, paprika, vinegar and lemon juice and pulse again until the mixture is smooth and vermillion. Now, slowly pour a steady stream of extra virgin olive oil into the blender as you are mixing – as you would when you make mayonnaise.

Serve the quails on a lake of romesco sauce with a simple salad or some steamed green beans.

KITCHEN-ADE

If you don't want to use quails, buy bone-in chicken breast instead and cook at the same temperature for 40–45 minutes.

SERVES 2

3 tsp sweet paprika
2 tbsp olive oil
leaves stripped from 3 or 4 sprigs of thyme
sea salt and freshly ground black pepper
2–4 quails, depending on their size and your appetite

For the romesco sauce

75g/3oz almonds, blanched and skins removed
75g/3oz stale ciabatta or any other crusty white loaf
2 medium ripe tomatoes, deseeded and finely chopped
225g/8oz roasted peppers in olive oil, drained and sliced
2 garlic cloves, chopped
½ tsp sweet paprika
1½ tbsp red wine vinegar
1 tbsp lemon juice
100ml/3½fl oz extra virgin olive oil

LADY & THE CLAM SPAGHETTI

Where clams are concerned, more is more, and if music is the food of love, the clattering of a generous amount of clams is as romantic a symphony as any. Do play on.

SERVES 2

30 clams in their shells
250g/9oz cherry tomatoes,
    halved
½ tsp chilli flakes
3 garlic cloves, sliced
sea salt and freshly ground
    black pepper
1 tsp caster sugar
extra virgin olive oil,
    to drizzle
250g/9oz spaghetti
½ onion, finely chopped
3 garlic cloves, chopped
zest and juice of ½ lemon
olive oil for frying
150ml/5fl oz white wine
1 handful of fresh flat-leaf
    parsley

KITCHEN-ADE
The saline juice of the clams flavours the sauce so well that you won't need to add any extra salt.

Spaghetti may not be a menu choice for a sweaty-palmed first date, but there is something childishly romantic about sharing a plate of it, hoping for a magical Lady and the Tramp moment. Disney fantasies aside, I have to admit I tend to cook this at home rather than ordering it in restaurants, where the disproportionate amount of pasta you get to clams can be disappointing.

Preheat the oven to 200°C/400°F/gas 6. Wash the clams in several changes of cold water, scrubbing them against each other to shake off any sediment. Get rid of any clams that will not close when you tap them lightly.

Arrange the tomatoes in a roasting tin. Add the chilli flakes and sliced garlic, season to taste with salt and pepper and sprinkle with the sugar and a drizzle of extra virgin olive oil. Roast them for 25 minutes until they have softened and caramelised slightly.

Bring a large pan of water to the boil and sprinkle in a little salt. Add the pasta and boil for 8–10 minutes or until al dente.

Meanwhile, fry the onion, chopped garlic and lemon zest in a generous slug of olive oil over a low heat. Once the onion has softened, pour in the wine, bring to the boil and cook until all the alcohol has evaporated. Throw in the tomatoes and stir for 2 minutes, then add the clams in all their clunking crustacean glory. Bring the liquid back up to the boil, cover the pan and cook for a further 3 minutes until the clams have opened up. Fish out and discard any that haven't opened. Stir in the parsley and lemon juice and serve the sauce spooned over the drained pasta.

SINFUL CHOCOLATE TRUFFLES

The path of true love doesn't always run smoothly, but a tray of melt-in-the-mouth, booze-laced truffles will certainly help it along.

Put the dark chocolate into a heatproof bowl. Heat the cream until it reaches boiling point, then pour it over the chocolate. Add the brandy and stir until smooth and glossy. Cover with cling film and refrigerate overnight.

Line a baking sheet with baking parchment. Take 2 teaspoonfuls of the chocolate mixture and roll into little balls. You have to work fast as it does melt and is a little messy, but remember you are not aiming for perfect circles here. Place the balls on the baking sheet and refrigerate again for 2 hours.

In a double boiler, melt the white chocolate. Set it aside to cool slightly, then dip each dark chocolate ball into the white chocolate, place back on the baking sheet and refrigerate for a further 2 hours to set. Once set, dust with cocoa powder. Eating just one is never enough.

MAKES 15

200g/7oz very good-quality
   dark chocolate, roughly
   chopped
125ml/4fl oz double cream
1 tbsp brandy
200g/7oz white chocolate,
   roughly chopped
good-quality cocoa powder,
   to dust

KITCHEN-ADE
For a nutty treat, skip the white chocolate and roll your truffles in 2 tablespoons of toasted crushed hazelnuts or almonds instead.

FIG TARTE TATIN

If you're looking for a boost in the bedroom department, forget a visit to the sex therapist and pay a visit to your greengrocer to pick up some figs.

**MAKES ABOUT 12
IRRESISTIBLE TARTS**

100g/3½oz unsalted butter
100g/3½oz caster sugar
3 cloves
1 star anise
8 figs, cut into fine segments
plain flour, to dust
250g/9oz ready-made puff
    pastry

These erotic fruits have long been a symbol of love and fertility, but for me the sex appeal of this recipe is obvious: jammy figs topped with melting sweet and spicy caramel and the flakiest puff pastry – it's like one arousing ingredient on top of another; surely you're tempted?

Preheat the oven to 190°C/375°F/gas 5 and line a 12-hole tart tin with baking parchment.

Melt the butter and sugar together with the cloves and star anise until they're golden and syrupy. Put 1 tablespoon of the syrup into each pie hole and then layer in the fig segments.

Roll out the pastry on a lightly floured surface until it is about 5mm/¼in thick, then cut out circles, wide enough to cover the figs and caramel in the pie tin. Place the pastry circles over the figs and carefully tuck in the edges.

Pop into the oven and bake until the pastry is cooked and golden – 12–15 minutes. Invert each little tart and serve immediately with a scoop of vanilla ice cream – there is something sensational about the combination of hot caramel and pastry with ice-cold ice cream.

FRENCH MARTINI JELLY & ICE CREAM

When it comes to the choice between a cocktail and a pudding, I always opt to cash in my calories on dessert.

SERVES 2

30g/generous 1oz caster sugar
30ml/generous 1fl oz water
3 sheets of leaf gelatine
30ml/generous 1fl oz raspberry liqueur, such as Chambord
125ml/scant 4fl oz pineapple juice
90ml/scant 3½fl oz vodka
100g/3½oz raspberries
sugared lemon rind and vanilla ice cream, to serve

With this very adult version of jelly and ice cream, there isn't a choice to be made. Here's how to have your cocktail, and eat it.

Put the sugar and water in a heavy-based saucepan over a low heat and cook until the sugar has dissolved. Bring it up to boiling point and then simmer until it has turned syrupy. Set it aside to cool.

Meanwhile, soak the gelatine in cold water for 6 minutes. Squeeze out the excess water and stir it into the sugar syrup along with the raspberry liqueur, pineapple juice and vodka.

Divide the raspberries between 2 martini glasses or teacups as I have here, pour in the liquid and place in the refrigerator for 6 hours to set. Serve with a twist of sugared lemon rind and vanilla ice cream.

CHOCOLATE-&-LIQUEUR-DIPPED STRAWBERRIES

If love was like it is in the movies, a plate of these strawberries would just be a scene from '9 ½ weeks' waiting to unfold.

The truth of the matter is that you'll be so lost in the delicious contrast between the dark chocolate and juicy strawberries, you'll barely notice your partner. But with just enough brandy to loosen your inhibitions, there is still hope. Lights, camera – ACTION!

Line a baking tray with baking parchment. Melt the chocolate and butter over a double boiler. Once it is molten, add the liqueur and cream and stir until luscious and smooth. Dip three-quarters of each strawberry into the chocolate, then transfer to the tray and leave to harden. Refrigerate to set further. Serve with a wink and a smile.

MAKES 12 TREATS

150g/5oz dark chocolate (at least 70% cocoa solids here)
1 large knob of unsalted butter
1 tbsp orange liqueur, such as Grand Marnier
1 tbsp double cream
12 strawberries

KITCHEN-ADE
Try varying the recipe by using white chocolate and rum instead.

LYCHEE JELLY WITH VANILLA PANNACOTTA

Are you really ready for this jelly? No party is complete without it.

SERVES 2

100g/3½oz lychees, stoned
3 sheets of leaf gelatine
250ml/8fl oz lychee or
    apple juice
25g/1oz caster sugar

For the vanilla pannacotta
2 sheets of leaf gelatine
175ml/6fl oz full-fat milk
175ml/6fl oz double cream
½ vanilla pod
1 tbsp caster sugar

The juicy exotic lychees in a just-set jelly, topped with creamy pannacotta that wobbles with a mere glance, is as pleasing to the eye as it is to the belly.

Place a single layer of lychees in the bottom of 2 dessert bowls or tumblers. Soak the gelatine in warm water for 5 minutes to soften.

Place one-third of the fruit juice in a saucepan along with the sugar and heat over a moderate heat until the sugar has dissolved. Next, add the gelatine, squeezing out the excess water, and stir over the heat until it has dissolved. Add the remaining juice and immediately pour it over the lychees. Refrigerate for about 6 hours until it is well set.

For the pannacotta, soak the gelatine leaves in a little warm water to soften. Meanwhile, place the milk, cream, vanilla pod and sugar into a pan and bring to a simmer – do not let it boil. Remove the vanilla pod, squeeze out the excess water from the gelatine and add to the pan. Take off the heat and stir again, until the gelatine has completely dissolved. Leave until cold, then pour over the lychee jelly and refrigerate for a further 2 hours or until it is just set.

RASPBERRY ROSE PAVLOVA

These light and airy rose meringues are a sure way to put the bloom back into your lover's cheeks.

The crisp yet chewy texture, perfumed floral flavour and layer of tart raspberries and voluptuous cream are an orgy of gastronomic pleasure.

Preheat the oven to 180°C/350°F/gas 4. Line a baking sheet with baking parchment. In a large bowl, beat the egg whites until they have the consistency of a melting Mr Whippy, then slowly add the sugar, a little at a time, until you have a glossy, satiny and stiffer egg white mix. Sprinkle the vanilla extract, rose water and vinegar into the bowl and fold in, being careful not to beat the air out of the egg whites.

Pipe or, if you like a more rustic meringue as I do, spoon the mixture onto baking parchment in two vaguely love-heart shapes. (I often draw the shapes on with a pencil just to give me a rough guideline, but I have to admit I sometimes find it difficult, as I did as an enthusiastic young colourer, to stay inside the lines.) You can also make different sized circles and layer them on top of each other to make an impressive tower.

Place the meringues in the oven and turn the heat down immediately to 150°C/300°F/gas 2. Cook for 55 minutes – the top should be set into a thin delicate shell while the inside should still be dreamily gooey. Leave the meringues to cool in the oven with the door open.

Once they are cool, invert the meringues onto a plate. Whip up the double cream until it is thick but still soft and then spoon onto each meringue. Finally, crown each meringue with a pile of raspberries. This is just a suggestion, but I have often found sticking a sparkler in your meringue, tacky as it may seem, somehow always makes your post-pudding entertaining go off with a bang!

SERVES 2

2 egg whites
125g/4oz caster sugar
1 tsp vanilla extract
2 tsp rose water
1 tsp white wine vinegar
150ml/5fl oz double cream
250g/9oz raspberries

KITCHEN-ADE
Work quickly once your egg white and sugar mixture is ready, so that your meringues don't wilt. If you're pressed for time, make them a day before and, once they have cooled completely, store in an airtight container.

CHAPTER TWELVE

Meet the parents

...And other awkward situations where you should let the food do the talking

We've all been there and done it – you know the old routine: 1) Hotfoot it to the über expensive deli. 2) Buy a selection of bank-breaking goodies. 3) Reheat. 4) Serve it up on your best china. 5) Smile graciously when complimented on your authentic Italian cooking. But here's the thing – that old trick's getting to be more see-through than last season's Chloe summer dress.

It's easy to watch luscious domestic goddess Nigella and hot-tempered hottie Gordon do their stuff on the box – but now's your chance to put what you've learnt into practice. It's your kitchen, so make the show your own!

Banish all thoughts of dinner party disasters and kitchen nightmares – you can be the hostess with the mostess. Plan ahead; add a few fail-safe recipes to your repertoire. You'll be surprised how much money you save skipping past the deli – treat yourself to some new shoes as an incentive – and anyhow, you can't keep your kitchen barricaded forever!

SOUTH INDIAN FISH CURRY & LEMON RICE

This South Indian-inspired curry is light, delicate and sophisticated.

SERVES 6

1kg/2¼lb firm white-fleshed
  fish fillets, such as
  monkfish, pollack, cod
  or sole, cut into
  bite-sized chunks
1 tsp turmeric
1 tsp sea salt
juice of ½ lemon

For the curry
3 tbsp vegetable oil
2 tsp mustard seeds
1 pinch of asafoetida
  (see page 183)
8 cloves, ground to a
  coarse powder
15–20 curry leaves
  (see page 183)
½ tsp cumin seeds
2 red onions, thinly sliced
  into crescents
sea salt
1 red chilli, deseeded and
  sliced
2 fingers of fresh root
  ginger, peeled and cut
  into fine matchsticks
½ tsp turmeric
1 tbsp caster sugar

There is no sinus-clearing heat here, just the sweet mellowness of rich coconut milk. Instead of loud spices, just the genteel tempering of nutty mustard seeds and aromatic curry leaves warmed through with cloves and ginger. No lurid day-glo sauce, just the pale sigh of golden turmeric. There is no dish that makes me more nostalgic about my holiday spent dreaming on the backwaters of Kerala than this one. This recipe is a favourite souvenir I share with friends again and again.

Put the fish into a mixing bowl, sprinkle with the turmeric and salt and squeeze the lemon juice over. Mix well to coat the fish pieces and leave to marinate for 30 minutes.

To make the curry, heat the vegetable oil in a large wok until smoking, then add the mustard seeds. As soon as they start popping, add the asafoetida, cloves and curry leaves. Stir briefly, then add the cumin, onions and a little salt to stop the onions browning. Fry over a gentle heat until the onions have softened and turned pale pink. Add the chilli and ginger and stir-fry for a few minutes more, then sprinkle in the turmeric and sugar and stir-fry for another minute. Whisk the tamarind into the coconut milk and pour the liquid into the pan along with the water. Bring the mixture up to the boil, then reduce the heat, add the fish and simmer gently for 5 minutes.

Meanwhile, cook the rice until it is tender and drain. In another pan, heat the oil in a pan and add the asafoetida, followed by the split black gram, chilli and mustard seeds. When these start popping, add the curry leaves, lemon zest and juice and turmeric. Stir the cooked rice into the pan, making sure the spices are evenly mixed through it.

Finally, add the prawns to the fish and cook for a further 3 minutes until the fish is cooked through and the prawns have turned pink. Remove from the heat, stir in the coriander and pour the lemon juice over the top. Serve immediately with a bowl of the lemon rice.

KITCHEN-ADE

Split black gram or lentils are cheap and readily available. They are sometimes called 'urad dal'. If you can't get hold of them, you can leave them out, but they give the rice a lovely nutty crunch.

3 tbsp tamarind concentrate
400ml/14fl oz coconut milk
500ml/18fl oz water
500g/1lb 2oz large raw
   prawns, peeled and
   deveined
1 small bunch of coriander,
   roughly chopped
juice of 1 large lemon

For the lemon rice

500g/1lb 2oz basmati rice
3 tbsp vegetable oil
1 pinch of asafoetida
2 heaped tbsp split black
   gram (see Kitchen-ade)
1 dried red chilli
1 tbsp mustard seeds
15 curry leaves
zest and juice of 1 lemon
½ tsp turmeric

SALT-CRUSTED SEA BASS WITH HONEY-ROASTED RADISHES

I first came across this ingenious way of cooking fish when I was in Sardinia. The fish would literally come out of the water, be packed in salt and get thrown on a barbecue.

SERVES 4

2kg/4½lb fine sea salt
zest of 2 lemons
3 tbsp chopped fresh
     rosemary leaves
3 tbsp chopped fresh
     thyme leaves
2 egg whites
60ml/generous 2fl oz water
1 lemon, cut into thick
     slices
1kg/2¼lb whole sea bass,
     scaled and gutted
extra virgin olive oil,
     to drizzle
2 tbsp chopped fresh flat-leaf
     parsley, to garnish

For the radishes
15–20 radishes, topped
     and tailed
a drizzle of olive oil
2 tbsp runny honey
sea salt and freshly ground
     black pepper

The salt back in England didn't seem to have the same staying power, so I added the egg whites and water to help it stick, and the addition of the lemon zest and herbs gives the fish a whisper of subtle flavour. The best part of this dish is the theatre of cracking away the salt to reveal the tenderest juicy fish, all accompanied by plenty of ooh and aahs from your guests.

Preheat the oven to 200°C/400°F/gas 6. Prepare the radishes. Pop them in a roasting tin, pour the olive oil, honey and seasoning over them and mix, making sure they are all well coated and glistening with the honey and oil. Put to one side.

Put the salt into a large mixing bowl and mix in the lemon zest and herbs. In a separate bowl, whisk the egg whites until they have almost doubled in size, then fold gently into the salt mixture. Mix in the water – you should now have the consistency of wet sand.

Pop the lemon slices into the fish and then start packing it with salt. I normally begin by placing half of the salt mixture on the bottom of a roasting tin, placing the fish on top of it and then packing the rest of the salt tightly over the top. The crust should be about 2cm/¾in thick all around and you needn't worry about covering the head and the tail of the fish.

Once the fish is tucked into its salty bed, put it into the oven. It should take between 40 and 45 minutes to cook. Halfway through the cooking time, put in the radishes and cook until pale pink and caramelised.

To test if the fish is cooked through, insert a skewer through the crust and into the centre of it – if your skewer comes out warm, it's ready to eat.

To serve, crack open the golden salt crust and peel away. Lift out the fillets, drizzle with some extra virgin olive oil and scatter on a little parsley.

ROAST BRILL WITH CARAMELISED LEMONS, FENNEL & CAPERS

You're usually a dial out and takeaway kind of girl, but this is the kind of delicious dinner that delivers in less than the usual 30 minutes it takes for the delivery boy to reach you.

SERVES 6

4 tbsp olive oil
2 fennel bulbs, each cut into
  6 wedges, fennel fronds
  reserved and chopped
1 lemon, cut into 6 wedges
2 tsp caster sugar
6 thick brill fillets
1 knob of unsalted butter
3 garlic cloves, sliced
3 tbsp capers
6 stalks of cherry tomatoes
  on the vine
1 heaped tsp fennel seeds
sea salt and freshly ground
  black pepper

The combination of thick meaty fish, caramelised fennel and lemon is, well, brill-iant! Don't expect tips, though – just smile graciously and accept your guests' glowing praise.

Preheat the oven to 200°C/400°F/gas 6. Heat 1 tablespoon of the olive oil in a pan over a medium flame. Add the fennel and lemon wedges, sprinkle with the sugar and cook until you have a deep caramelised brown colour on the first side. Turn the fennel wedges and caramelise the other side.

Score the skin of the fish at 2.5cm/1in intervals and make sure it is completely dry – this helps the skin to go very crispy. Heat a knob of butter in a pan with the remaining olive oil, to stop it burning, and cook the fish, skin-side down, for 3 minutes until the skin has crisped up.

Season the fish generously on both sides and place in a roasting tin, skin-side down. Arrange the garlic, capers, tomatoes, caramelised fennel and lemon over the fish. Sprinkle with the fennel seeds and extra seasoning and roast for 10–15 minutes or until the fish is opaque and cooked through. Scatter with the reserved fennel fronds and serve immediately.

BUTTERFLIED LEG OF LAMB

WITH A SPICY YOGHURT AND HERB CRUST

Roast dinners can be a palaver, but although this one looks like you've spent the day slaving over it, it's hardly what I'd call labour intensive.

SERVES 6

1.5kg/3¼lb leg of lamb –
    get your butcher to take
    out the bone so that the
    meat lies flat like a page
sea salt
6 garlic cloves
1 bunch of fresh mint,
    chopped
1 bunch of fresh coriander,
    chopped
400g/14oz natural yoghurt
2 tsp paprika
2 tsp ground roasted
    cumin seeds
2 tsp ground roasted
    coriander seeds
juice and zest of 1 large
    lemon
½ tsp saffron strands
    strands pounded in
    2 tsp warm water
1 tsp coarsely ground
    black pepper

Simply whiz up your marinade in a blender, coat the lamb and then throw in the oven an hour before you're ready to eat. Also, cooking the lamb with the bone taken out like this means it'll cook quickly, evenly and be a piece of cake to carve.

Trim any excess fat from the lamb and then sprinkle it liberally with sea salt. To make the marinade, chop the garlic and herbs finely, then mix with the yoghurt, spices, lemon zest and juice, saffron, pepper and salt. Smear the lamb with the yoghurt mix and leave to marinate overnight or for at least 4 hours – this will give you the most tender melt-in-the-mouth lamb ever, as the lemon and yoghurt tenderise any sinews.

When you are ready to cook, preheat the oven to 200°C/400°F/gas 6. Place the lamb directly on the oven rack, with a tray underneath to catch any dripping juices. Cook for about 45 minutes for medium meat, or about 1 hour if you like it well done. Turn the lamb halfway through the cooking time and baste with the juices from the pan.

Once cooked, remove your lamb from the oven, pop it in a warm place and leave it to rest for at least 10 minutes before carving.

SEVEN-SPICE PORK CHOPS
WITH APPLE, MINT & MANGO CHUTNEY

Marinate these chops for as long a possible – a good 6 hours or overnight is what I recommend.

SERVES 6

3 fat garlic cloves, roughly chopped

2 green chillies (deseeded if you don't
    want it too spicy), roughly chopped

7.5cm/3in knob of fresh root ginger,
    peeled and roughly chopped

¼ tsp whole cloves

1 tbsp coriander seeds

5 green cardamom pods

1 tbsp whole black peppercorns

1 tbsp cumin seeds

1 star anise

8 heaped tbsp natural yoghurt

½ tsp turmeric

1 tsp sea salt

½ tsp red chilli powder

juice of ½ lemon

6 pork chops

For the chutney

1 Bramley apple, peeled and roughly
    chopped

1 mango, peeled and roughly chopped

1 small onion, roughly chopped

1 green chilli (deseeded if you don't
    want it too spicy), roughly chopped

1 bunch of fresh mint, roughly torn

sea salt

2 tsp caster sugar

The yoghurt helps to tenderise the meat, leaving it sticky and toothsome with a good golden rind of fat. The accompanying chutney gives a fresh piquancy to the spicy meat – but don't just reserve it for chops, it's excellent on a cheeseboard or in sandwiches too.

Put the garlic, chillies and ginger into a food processor and blitz to a paste, or pound in a pestle and mortar. Toast all the whole spices in the dry pan until aromatic, then crush in a pestle and mortar until you have a coarse powder. Combine the spice mix with the yoghurt, turmeric, salt, red chilli powder, lemon juice and the garlic, ginger and chilli paste. Smear it all over the pork chops and leave to marinate overnight or for at least 6 hours.

You can make the chutney in advance, as it keeps for a week in the fridge. Put the apple, mango, onion, chilli and mint into a food processor and blitz to a fine paste. Season with salt and stir in the sugar.

Heat a griddle pan or a grill to medium and cook the chops for 6 minutes on each side or until cooked through, basting with the excess marinade as you cook. Serve with the chutney and some boiled new potatoes.

LAMB BIRYANI

Don't be put off by the humungous list of ingredients here – most of them are spices.

If you aren't keen on the grinding involved (I find it therapeutic), by all means buy a ready-made spice mix. Shan (a brand that's an Indian housewife's storecupboard secret) do excellent ones. For just under a pound, all the laborious grinding has been done for you. They're readily available in Indian supermarkets or online at www.spicesofindia.co.uk. Look out for the Sindhi and Bombay Biryani mixes.

First make the mint raita. Simply whisk together all the ingredients except the cumin. Heat a pan. When it is very hot, sprinkle in the cumin and as soon as it becomes aromatic take it off the heat and sprinkle it over the yoghurt mix. Refrigerate until ready to serve.

Now to the biryani. Put the onion chunks, garlic, ginger and chillies into a food processor and blitz to a paste. Fry the paste in a slug of vegetable oil over a medium heat for 8–10 minutes or until brown and well cooked.

Put the lamb into a marinating dish. Add the fried onion paste, turmeric, yoghurt and lime juice and leave to marinate for a few hours or overnight.

Wash the rice in several changes of water. Add the salt to a pan of water and bring to the boil. Add the rice, cinnamon, peppercorns, cardamom pods, cloves and cumin seeds and cook for about 10 minutes until the rice is half cooked – it should still have bite. Drain well and then spread over a large tray to cool. Crush the saffron in the warm water, mix well and then sprinkle over the rice. The aim is to get contrasting crocus-stained rice and pearly white rice. Finally, sprinkle with the rose water.

SERVES 6

2 large red onions, 1 chopped into chunks and 1 finely sliced into crescents
5 fat garlic cloves, roughly chopped
7.5cm/3in knob of fresh root ginger, peeled and roughly chopped
2 green chillies (deseeded if you don't want it too spicy), roughly chopped
vegetable oil for frying
750g/1lb 10oz cubed shoulder of lamb
½ tsp turmeric
250g/8oz natural yoghurt
juice of 1 lime
4 ripe tomatoes, chopped
2 tbsp tomato purée
10 dried apricots
5 tbsp chopped fresh mint
5 tbsp chopped fresh coriander
8 small new potatoes, parboiled and cut into bite-sized chunks
mint raita, to serve (see page 273)

Preheat the oven to 170°C/325°F/gas 3. Using a spice grinder or a pestle and mortar, grind all the spices for the spice mix together into a coarse blend.

In a large frying pan, heat a little vegetable oil and fry the sliced onion until golden. Remove from the oil with a slotted spoon and drain on kitchen paper. Add the marinated lamb and all the marinating juices to the pan and fry for about 10 minutes. Add the tomatoes, tomato purée, apricots and spice mix and mix well, then cover and simmer for about 30 minutes, until the meat is tender and the sauce has thickened and reduced. Sprinkle the mint and coriander in and stir.

Put half the meat into a deep casserole dish and top with half the rice. Scatter half the fried onions on and then push half the potatoes into the rice. Top with the remaining lamb and a final layer of rice and onions, pushing the last of the potatoes into the rice. Dot the surface of the rice with a little ghee and a final sprinkling of rose water. Cover the biryani with a layer of greased kitchen foil and then top with a snug-fitting lid to ensure none of the steam escapes – this is what will make your rice lovely and fluffy.

Bake in the oven for 40 minutes until it is fragrant and perfectly cooked. Garnish with the hard-boiled eggs and coriander and serve with the mint raita.

For the rice

500g/1lb 2oz basmati rice
2 tsp sea salt
2 cinnamon sticks
1 tsp whole black peppercorns
6 green cardamom pods, bruised
½ tsp whole cloves
2 tsp cumin seeds
1 large pinch of saffron strands
4 tbsp warm water
2 tbsp rose water, plus extra
   to sprinkle
ghee, to sprinkle

For the spice mix

1 tsp cumin seeds
½ tsp whole black peppercorns
1 dried red chilli
6 cloves
6 green cardamom pods
½ tsp ground cinnamon
½ tsp freshly grated nutmeg
½ tsp ground mace
1 tbsp mango powder (amchur,
   see page 32)

For the garnish

3 hard-boiled eggs, cut into quarters
a sprinkle of coriander

For mint raita

400g/14oz natural yoghurt
1 large handful of fresh mint,
   finely chopped
1 green chilli (deseeded if you don't
   want it too spicy), finely chopped
½ onion, finely chopped
juice of ½ lime
sea salt and freshly ground
   black pepper
½ tsp toasted cumin

HOT SAUSAGE ROAST
WITH SWEET & SOUR SHALLOT GRAVY

You don't mind cooking – it's the Everest-sized washing-up mountain that drives you crazy.

SERVES 4

4 medium waxy potatoes
20 baby shallots or silver-
   skin pickling onions
4 garlic cloves, finely
   chopped
olive oil, to drizzle
sea salt and freshly ground
   black pepper
250g/9oz chestnut
   mushrooms, halved
8 good-quality sausages of
   your choice
a few sprigs of thyme
250ml/8fl oz red wine
1 tbsp brown sugar
6 tbsp balsamic vinegar

Good to know then that this sticky sausage supper is all cooked in one pot, so you can relax and enjoy your guests dishing their latest dirt, rather than doing the dirty dishes. This makes an ideal after-work supper.

Preheat the oven to 200°C/400°F/gas 6. Scrub the potatoes but don't peel them, then cut into thick slices. Put the potatoes, onions and garlic into a large roasting tin with a drizzle of olive oil. Season generously with salt and pepper and mix well. Put into the oven and roast for 25 minutes, then add the mushrooms, turning the vegetables to make sure the mushrooms get a good coating of the garlicky olive oil. Lay the sausages on top of the mushrooms, top with the thyme sprigs and baste with the oily juices of the vegetables. Roast for another 20 minutes, then turn the sausages and cook for a final 20 minutes.

Once the sausages are cooked, transfer them along with the potatoes and mushrooms to a hot plate and keep warm while you make the gravy. Leave the onions in the pan but remove and discard the thyme sprigs. Put the roasting tin on the hob and deglaze the pan by pouring in the wine – scrape off all the caramelised bits in the bottom of the pan for extra flavour. Let the wine bubble and reduce by half, then add the sugar and balsamic vinegar and keep stirring until you have a thick, sticky gravy. Drizzle over the sausages and vegetables and serve immediately.

CRISPY FIVE-SPICE DUCK BREASTS & PAK CHOI WITH CHILLI & GARLIC CONFETTI

On the rare occasion there is any left over, I tear it into shards and roll it into warm tortillas with splinters of cucumber and spring onion.

SERVES 6

1 heaped tbsp ground ginger

2 heaped tbsp Chinese
   five-spice powder

1 tsp sweet paprika

2 tbsp olive oil

1 tsp sesame oil

4 tbsp dark soy sauce

4 tbsp maple syrup

6 duck breasts

For the pak choi

vegetable oil for frying

7 garlic cloves, 4 finely
   sliced and 3 chopped

2 red chillies (deseeded if
   you don't want it too
   spicy), finely sliced on
   the diagonal

500g/1lb 2oz baby pak choi

2 tbsp chicken stock

2 tbsp light soy sauce

1 tsp sesame oil

1 tsp caster sugar

The Chinese have duck-roasting down to a fine art – their rigorous method of pumping air into the duck to separate the skin from the flesh, soaking it and then hanging it to dry results in the perfectly brown bird with crackling skin. This version gives more-ishly crunchy skin and succulent gamey meat with considerably less effort.

Preheat the oven to 200°C/375°F/gas 6. Combine the ginger, five-spice powder and paprika in a bowl and then whisk in the oils, soy sauce and maple syrup.

Using a sharp knife, score the skin of the duck breasts in a criss-cross pattern, making sure you don't cut into the flesh. This helps the skin really crisp up. Heat a large pan until very hot and place the duck breasts, skin-side down, in it and cook for 3 minutes to draw out the fat. Remove the duck and drain the fat. Put the duck back into the hot pan, flesh-side down, and baste each breast with half the marinade. Cook for a further 3 minutes, then place the duck breasts on a wire rack in a roasting pan and baste again. Cook in the oven for 5 minutes on each side, basting as you go.

To prepare the pak choi, put 1cm/½in of vegetable oil into a wok and fry the sliced garlic and chillies until golden. Drain on kitchen paper. Remove most of the oil from the pan, leaving about 3 tbsp, and add the chopped garlic. When it is golden and aromatic, throw in the pak choi and stir-fry for 1 minute. The aim is to wilt the leaves but keep the stems crunchy. Pour in the chicken stock, soy sauce, sesame oil and sugar and cook again for a further minute. Sprinkle in the reserved garlic and chillies.

Take the duck out of the oven and let it rest for 5 minutes. Slice it and serve with a nest of pak choi.

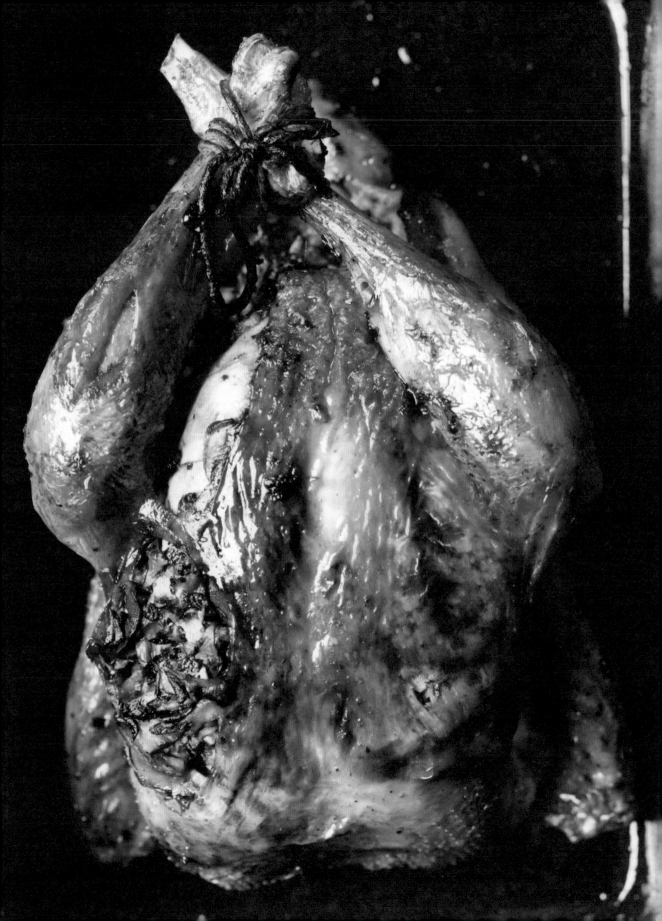

LEMON & GARLIC ROAST CHICKEN
WITH MUSHROOM & CORIANDER STUFFING

A well-roasted chicken is more than a simple pleasure: it is magnificence on a platter.

The nut-brown bird, with skin as crisp and crackly as taffeta gauze, the malleable flesh as easy to carve as butter, is a sight for your guests to behold and salivate over. If your bird is a good-quality, happy, organic one, a simple seasoning of salt and pepper will make it tasty enough, but I love this stuffing of pungent garlic, woody mushrooms and sharp lemon, all brightened up with fragrant coriander.

Preheat the oven to 190°C/375°F/gas 5. Wash your chicken inside and out and pat dry with kitchen paper. Massage the skin of the chicken, pinching and loosening it over the breast area, then push your fingers under the breast skin and pull it away from the breast completely, but don't tear it. Season the chicken generously with salt and pepper inside and out and baste generously all over with the olive oil or softened butter.

To make the stuffing, mix the garlic with the mushrooms, coriander, butter, lemon zest and juice and seasoning. Stuff this mixture into the space under the breast skin, making sure you push and pack it in well. This will keep the breast meat really moist. Stuff any remaining mixture inside the chicken with the lemon halves inside too for extra flavour.

Place the chicken on its breast, so it is lying legs up, in a roasting tin and roast for 30 minutes. Remove from the oven and carefully turn it onto its back, then baste with the tray juices and roast for a further 35 minutes. The trick to roasting it upside down like this is that the juices from the fatty skin underneath the chicken drip down and baste the meat, ensuring the breast meat will be moist and succulent.

Once it's cooked, leave to stand for 10–15 minutes. Carve and enjoy with a glutton's portion of golden roast potatoes.

SERVES 4

2kg/4½lb whole chicken
olive oil or 1 tbsp unsalted
    butter, softened, to baste

For the stuffing
1 whole bulb of garlic,
    peeled and chopped
250g/9oz assorted
    mushrooms, sliced
1 large handful of fresh
    coriander, chopped
100g/3½oz unsalted butter,
    softened
zest and juice of 1 lemon
sea salt and freshly ground
    black pepper
1 lemon, halved

FRAGRANT CHICKEN CURRY

WITH STAR ANISE & LACE PANCAKES

I love the cuisine of Malaysia – it's a melting pot of influences from all corners of Asia.

SERVES 6

1 heaped tbsp ghee or 3 tbsp vegetable oil

2 large red onions, sliced into fine
  crescents

1 tsp cumin seeds

6 garlic cloves, roughly chopped

2 red chillies (deseeded if you don't want
  it too spicy), roughly chopped

7.5cm/3in knob of fresh root ginger,
  peeled and roughly chopped

sea salt

1 curl of cinnamon

1 stalk of curry leaves (see page 183)

3 tbsp mild or medium Madras curry
  powder

2 star anise

1 × 400g tin of chopped tomatoes

1 × 400ml tin of coconut milk

400ml/14fl oz water

3 small to medium potatoes, cut
  into quarters

8 chicken thighs, skinned

juice of 1 lime

**For the lace pancakes –
makes about 12**

250g/9oz plain flour

1 tsp sea salt

½ tsp turmeric

2 large eggs, beaten

250ml/8fl oz full-fat or semi-skimmed
  milk

250ml/8fl oz evaporated milk

This Indo-Malay curry is my absolute favourite and breathes life into chicken, which can sometimes be a little bland. You can make your own curry powder, but a mild to medium Madras powder does the trick very well. Mop up the rich soupy curry sauce with the delicate lacy pancakes. They look like cut-out paper snowflakes or a delicate gothic cobweb and are often served at Malaysian weddings. They're as easy to make as regular pancakes, with no flipping involved.

Heat a large pan and melt the ghee or oil. (You can use ordinary vegetable oil, but ghee gives the curry sauce a rich melting deliciousness.) Once it is hot, add the onions and cumin and fry until it is golden brown. Meanwhile, put the garlic, chillies and ginger into a food processor and blitz to a fine paste. Add this to the golden onions along with some salt, the cinnamon, curry leaves, curry powder and star anise. Fry the spices until aromatic – about 3 minutes, then pour in the tomatoes. Cook for 3–4 minutes, then pour in the coconut milk and water. Bring the sauce to the boil, then simmer it for 3 minutes. Toss in the potatoes and chicken. Bring the sauce to a boil again, then lower the heat, cover the pan and simmer on a low heat for about 25 minutes until the chicken is cooked. Take off the heat and squeeze the lime juice over before serving.

To make the lace pancakes, sift the flour, salt and turmeric into a large mixing bowl. In another bowl, whisk together the eggs, milk and evaporated milk and then slowly whisk the liquid ingredients into the flour until you have a smooth, velvet batter.

Lightly oil and heat a non-stick pan. Pour your batter mix into one of those cheap plastic ketchup bottles with a funnel top you see in greasy spoons. Now squirt the batter in a lacy pattern all over the base of the pan – it should look like a web or like Mr Squiggle – and cook it for 2 minutes until golden brown. Fold the pancake into quarters, or roll like a spring roll. These pancakes are cooked on one side only – the inside should be just set. Repeat with the remaining batter. Serve with the curry.

DILL CRÊPES WITH GREEN VEGETABLES, FETA & BÉCHAMEL SAUCE

I simply flip over crêpes — they're edible muslin rags, delicately laced at the edges. A simple culinary pleasure.

SERVES 4–6

For the crêpe batter
150g/5oz plain flour
150ml/5fl oz full-fat milk
150ml/5fl oz water
3 large eggs
2 tbsp melted unsalted
    butter, cooled
sea salt
3 tbsp finely chopped
    fresh dill
a little unsalted butter
    for frying

For the béchamel sauce
450ml/15fl oz full-fat milk
1 onion studded with
    6 cloves
1 bay leaf
12 peppercorns
1 blade of mace
50g/2oz unsalted butter
25g/1oz plain flour
sea salt and freshly ground
    black pepper
freshly grated nutmeg

It's a great shame then that they hardly surface in the British kitchen, apart from the token Shrove Tuesday. I eat them passionately whether they're sweet or savoury, and love how there is so much you can do with them beyond the legendary crêpes Suzette. They can be served for breakfast, lunch or dinner and whipped up at a moment's notice, the ingredients waiting like dependable friends in the pantry. These stuffed crêpes are my alternative to the regular vegetable lasagne.

To prepare the crêpe batter, put the flour, milk, water, eggs, melted butter and salt into a bowl. Mix with an electric whisk for 30 seconds, then stir in the dill. Chill in the fridge for 30 minutes.

Heat a 15–18cm/6–7in non-stick frying pan over a moderate heat until hot. Brush the pan lightly with the butter, heat until hot but not smoking, then remove from the heat. Stir the batter and pour a small ladleful into the pan. Tilt and rotate the pan quickly to cover the bottom with a layer of batter. Return the pan to the heat, loosen the edges of the crêpe with a spatula and cook for 1 minute, or until the top appears almost dry. Turn the crêpe (or flip it if you're supple of wrist), cook the other side lightly and transfer the crêpe to a plate. Make crêpes with the remaining batter in the same manner, brushing the pan lightly with butter as necessary.

Preheat the oven to 180°C/350°F/gas 4. To make the béchamel sauce, place the milk, onion, bay leaf, peppercorns and mace in a saucepan over a medium heat and bring to the boil, stirring continuously, then simmer gently, stirring, for 5 minutes. Remove from the heat, strain and discard any solids.

Wash the saucepan and then melt the butter in it over a low heat, making sure it doesn't burn or brown. Sprinkle in the flour, a little at a time, stirring vigorously with a wooden spoon – you should now have a thick glossy paste. Whisk in the milk, a little at a time, stirring as you go to avoid any lumps. Bring to the boil, then simmer the sauce for 5 minutes, season and stir in the nutmeg.

The pancake filling is extremely simple – heat the olive oil in a frying pan, then add the sliced onions, garlic, mushrooms and broccoli and cook until the onions are soft and the mushrooms have just begun to colour. Next, tumble in the olives and artichokes, season and stir in the Worcestershire sauce.

Spread 3 tablespoons of the filling on each crêpe, crumble on some feta and roll them up. Arrange the crêpes, seam-sides down, in a shallow baking dish just large enough to hold them in one layer. Pour the béchamel sauce over them, sprinkle with the Parmesan cheese and bake for 25 minutes until golden and bubbling.

For the filling and topping

1 tbsp olive oil

1 red onion, sliced

2 garlic cloves, chopped

250g/9oz chestnut
mushrooms, halved

150g/5oz broccoli, cut into
small florets

20 kalamata olives

290g jar of artichokes hearts
in olive oil, drained

2 tbsp Worcestershire sauce

150g/5oz feta cheese,
crumbled

50g/2oz Parmesan cheese,
grated

AUBERGINE & GOAT'S CHEESE PARCELS

These light refreshing parcels are a gift to vegetarian guests in particular.

They look beautiful and taste of holidays in the Mediterranean. For an Italian flavour, use buffalo mozzarella in place of goat's cheese.

Cut the aubergines lengthways into 5mm/¼in slices. Discard the first and last slices. You should aim to have 16 slices.

Bring a large pan of water to the boil and boil the aubergines for 2–3 minutes. Drain, then pat dry with kitchen paper or a tea towel, pressing hard to squeeze out as much of the excess water as you can without tearing the slices.

Place one slice on a chopping board vertically and place a second slice across the middle of it horizontally, to make a cross shape. Layer a basil leaf, tomato slice, pepper strip, goat's cheese slice and seasoning in the middle and then fold in the ends of the aubergine to form a parcel. Repeat until you have 8 parcels. Once all the parcels are ready, heat a little olive oil in a pan and gently fry the parcels on both sides until they are golden brown and cooked through – 5–6 minutes.

Combine all the ingredients for the dressing. Drizzle the aubergine parcels with the dressing, garnish with basil leaves and serve immediately.

SERVES 4

2 large aubergines, trimmed
8 large fresh basil leaves,
    plus extra to garnish
2 plum tomatoes, sliced
    into at least 8 slices
    (excluding the ends)
1 red pepper, roasted,
    skinned and cut into
    8 strips
225g/8oz goat's cheese,
    sliced in 8 slices
sea salt and freshly ground
    black pepper
olive oil for frying

For the dressing
4 tbsp olive oil
1 tbsp fresh pesto
    (see page 40)
1 tbsp lemon juice

WILD MUSHROOM ARANCINI

I first started making these fist-sized balls of gooey rice to use up leftover risotto, but they are so good, it's worth going to the trouble of cooking risotto just to make them. Make smaller gobstopper-sized ones as a canapé or starter.

SERVES 6

30g/generous 1oz dried porcini
 mushrooms
500ml/18fl oz boiling water
30g/generous 1oz unsalted butter
200g/7oz wild mushrooms
800ml/scant 1½ pints chicken
 or vegetable stock, including
 the liquid from the porcini
 mushrooms
1 small onion, chopped
2 garlic cloves, chopped
zest of 1 lemon
350g/12oz arborio rice
150ml/5fl oz white wine
50g/2oz Parmesan cheese,
 grated
1 handful of chopped fresh
 flat-leaf parsley
4 eggs
100g/3½oz panko breadcrumbs
 (see page 80) or white
 breadcrumbs
olive oil for shallow-frying
freshly ground black pepper

To serve

romesco sauce (see page 247)
rocket salad

Soak the porcini mushrooms in the boiling water for 5 minutes. Strain and reserve the liquid, then chop them roughly. Melt about one-third of the butter in a frying pan and sauté the wild mushrooms until golden. Stir in the porcini mushrooms and fry again for a further 2 minutes. Set aside.

Top up the reserved porcini liquid with vegetable or chicken stock, put into a saucepan and keep on a low simmer.

Melt the remaining butter in a pan over a gentle heat and sauté the onion until pale but soft. Stir in the garlic and lemon zest and fry for a further 2 minutes. Sprinkle in the rice and fry over a medium heat until it turns translucent at the edges. Pour in the wine and stir, letting it bubble until it has almost disappeared. Start adding the hot stock, a little at a time, stirring the risotto constantly, making sure the liquid has been absorbed before adding the next ladleful. Stir in the reserved mushrooms and a good grind of pepper with the last ladle of stock. When the stock has been absorbed, sprinkle in the Parmesan cheese and parsley and leave to cool.

Preheat the oven to 180°C/350°F/gas 4. Beat 2 eggs and pour them into the risotto, stirring well, then leave to rest for 10 minutes.

Beat the remaining eggs in a shallow bowl and place the breadcrumbs in a plate. Make tennis ball-sized balls of the risotto, packing them tightly, then dip in the beaten egg and roll them in the breadcrumb mixture to coat. Repeat until you have 12 balls.

Shallow-fry in a little olive oil, 3 at a time, until they are golden brown all over. Transfer to a baking tray and cook in the oven for 15 minutes until warmed through. Serve with a helping of romesco sauce and a simple rocket salad.

CAULIFLOWER MANCHURIAN

There's more to a head of cauliflower than cauliflower cheese. Give it some cauli-power with this Indo-Chinese-inspired curry.

SERVES 6

groundnut oil for shallow- and
   deep-frying (see Cook's Notes, page 12)
1 medium cauliflower, cut into
   small florets
75g/3oz sesame seeds
rice, to serve

For the batter

3 tbsp cornflour
150g/5oz plain flour
4 garlic cloves, roughly chopped
2 green chillies (deseeded if you don't
   want it too spicy), roughly chopped
5cm/2in knob of fresh root ginger,
   peeled and roughly chopped
¼ tsp red chilli powder

sea salt
1 tsp Chinese five-spice powder

For the sauce

1 green and 1 red pepper, each deseeded
   and roughly chopped
3 garlic cloves, chopped
1 red onion, roughly chopped
5 spring onions, roughly chopped
5 tbsp tomato ketchup
2 tbsp light soy sauce
1 tbsp caster sugar
juice of ½ lemon
1 tsp rice vinegar
1½ tbsp sambal oelek (Indonesian spicy
   sauce) or chilli sauce
1 tsp Chinese five-spice powder

When I'm entertaining, I fry the cauliflower and make the sauce in advance. Warm the battered florets through in a 180°C/350°F/gas 4 oven and heat the sauce on your hob.

For the batter, sift the cornflour and plain flour into a bowl. In a food processor, blitz the garlic, chillies and ginger to a paste, then stir into the flours. Sprinkle in the chilli powder, salt to taste and five-spice and stir again. Add enough water to make a thick batter.

Heat the groundnut oil until very hot, then lower the heat to medium. Dip the cauliflower in the batter and roll it in the sesame seeds, then deep-fry until golden brown. Drain on kitchen paper to remove excess oil.

To make the sauce, heat 2 tablespoons of groundnut oil in a pan. When it's hot, toss in the peppers, garlic and onions and stir-fry for 3 minutes. Pour in the ketchup, soy, sugar, lemon juice, rice vinegar and sambal oelek or chilli sauce and sprinkle in the five-spice powder. Mix well and bring to a simmer. Pour the sauce over the cauliflower and serve with rice.

PINEAPPLE UPSIDE-DOWN PUDDING

The sunshine yellow cheeriness of pineapple, the cheeky wink of a trashy but necessary glacé cherry, glistening like a stripper's nipple, and the spicy warmth of this sponge is a combination sent from dessert heaven.

MAKES 8

65g/2½oz caster sugar
125ml/4fl oz water
8 pineapple rings
8 glacé cherries
200ml/7fl oz vegetable oil
175g/6oz golden caster sugar
4 eggs
1 tsp vanilla extract
zest of 1 lime
¼ tsp sea salt
1 pinch of ground cinnamon
75g/3oz fine semolina
2 tsp baking powder
125g/4oz ground almonds
honey, vanilla ice cream or
    custard, to serve

Preheat the oven to 170°C/325°F/gas 3 and line the base of eight 250ml/8fl oz ramekins with baking parchment.

Place the caster sugar and water in a heavy-based pan and stir over a moderate heat until the sugar has dissolved. Bring to the boil and then simmer until it turns into a dark amber caramel. Pour into the ramekins and carefully place a pineapple ring in each on the caramel. Place a cherry in the centre of each pineapple ring.

Whisk the vegetable oil, golden caster sugar, eggs, vanilla, lime zest and salt in a bowl until combined, then add the cinnamon, semolina, baking powder and ground almonds. Mix well to combine, then pour into the moulds. Bake for 25 minutes, then leave to stand for 10–15 minutes.

Invert the puddings onto serving plates and serve with a drizzle of honey, a scoop of vanilla ice cream or lashings of custard – the choice is yours.

MARGARITA SYRUP CAKE

You're still living down the previous year's holiday shame after one too many margaritas. Now there's a safer way of mixing a margarita — it involves cake batter.

SERVES 8

125g/4oz unsalted butter, softened
150g/5oz caster sugar
250g/9oz yoghurt
2 tbsp tequila
3 eggs, separated
zest of 1 lime
100g/3½oz self-raising flour
100g/3½oz fine semolina
1 tsp baking powder
50g/2oz ground almonds

For the syrup
75g/3oz caster sugar
juice and zest of ½ lime
1 tbsp water
4 tsp tequila
2 tsp Cointreau

Stick to dazzling your guests with your dessert rather than a repeat of last year's holiday performance.

Preheat the oven to 180°C/350°F/gas 4. Line a 20cm/8in cake tin with baking parchment.

Cream the butter and sugar together until the mixture is light and fluffy. Whisk in the yoghurt, tequila, egg yolks and lime zest and beat until you have a smooth batter. Sift in the flour, semolina and baking powder and stir well, making sure all the ingredients are well combined. Finally, stir in the ground almonds.

In a separate bowl, whisk up the egg whites until you have soft peaks and then, using a metal spoon, fold into the cake batter, being careful not to knock out the air from the egg whites. Bake in the oven for 50 minutes or until golden and cooked through.

To make the syrup, combine the sugar, lime juice, lime zest and water in a saucepan and heat over a low heat, stirring until the sugar has dissolved. Take off the heat and stir in the tequila and Cointreau.

Using a skewer, pierce several holes over the surface of the cake. Pour the syrup over the cake and leave it to absorb. Serve with a drizzle of cream and a twist of lime.

SWISS ROLL SUMMER BERRY TRIFLE WITH ROSÉ JELLY

I have a girlish fondness for trifles – it's their layer upon layer of frothy cream, cold custard and wibbly jelly that makes me think of wedding dresses.

I'm not a fussy trifler – I'll happily eat them made out of a packet, festooned with fake cream and chocolate sprinkles, or spoon a sherry-sodden portion from a nana's cut-glass bowl. But if trifles really were wedding gowns, this one would be a Vera Wang creation.

Make the jelly first. Heat 200ml/7fl oz of the wine with the sugar over a medium heat and stir until the sugar has dissolved. Add the berries and simmer over a low heat for 3–4 minutes, then take off the heat.

Meanwhile, soak the gelatine leaves in cold water for 5 minutes or until they are soft. Squeeze out the excess water and stir into the berry syrup until dissolved. Pour this mixture into a glass bowl and top up with the remaining wine. Cool and refrigerate for 4–6 hours or overnight to set.

To make the custard, beat together the eggs and sugar. Gently heat the cream and milk with the vanilla pod until you reach simmering point. Strain the mixture over the eggs and sugar and stir to make custard. Cool and refrigerate.

To assemble the trifle, slice the Swiss roll and arrange it on the base and around the inside of a large glass serving bowl. Turn the jelly out onto a board and chop with a sharp knife, then scatter it over the Swiss roll. Pour the cooled custard over the jelly and return it to the fridge until cold.

For the topping, whip the cream to soft peaks with the sugar and spoon over the custard in dreamy mounds. Decorate with the fresh berries and a scattering of toasted almonds.

SERVES 8–10

1 large chocolate Swiss roll

For the jelly
350ml/12fl oz sparkling rosé wine
175g/6oz caster sugar
500g/1lb 2oz frozen berries, such as raspberries and blackberries
5 sheets of leaf gelatine

For the custard
6 large eggs
150g/5oz caster sugar
300ml/10fl oz double cream
300ml/10fl oz full-fat milk
1 vanilla pod

For the topping
300ml/10fl oz double cream
1 tbsp caster sugar
150g/5oz raspberries
150g/5oz blackberries
30g/generous 1oz toasted flaked almonds

WHITE CHOCOLATE & CARDAMOM MOUSSE WITH PISTACHIO PRALINE

If love could be spooned, it would be like white chocolate mousse: perfect, pristine, comforting and smooth.

The frothy, sweet chocolate will make you giddy. The spicy cardamom will make your heart race. The splinters of praline will allow you to take the rough with the smooth. And although a broken heart lies at the bottom of an empty dish, you know you can mend it by making some more.

Lay a sheet of baking parchment over a baking sheet and sprinkle on a thin layer of the pistachios. Heat the sugar and water to make a caramel, stirring continuously until it becomes a beautiful amber colour. At this point, take it off the heat and pour it over the pistachios, making sure it is a glassy, thin, fragile layer.

Combine the cream and cardamoms in a saucepan and place over a low heat. Take it off the heat just before it gets to boiling point and set aside to cool.

Melt the chocolate over a double boiler until it's glossy and molten. Take it off the heat and pour in the cream through a sieve to strain the cardamom pods. In another bowl, whisk up the egg whites until they form stiff peaks. Gently but thoroughly fold into the chocolate mixture. Pour into either one large bowl or 6–8 dessert glasses and refrigerate to set for at least 3 hours.

Once it is set, smash the praline into large shards by striking it once through the middle with the end of a rolling pin. Push a shard of praline into the centre of each mousse and serve.

SERVES 6–8

For the praline
50g/2oz shelled pistachio
    nuts, roughly chopped
100g/3½oz caster sugar
5 tbsp water

For the mousse
300ml/10fl oz double cream
6 green cardamom pods,
    crushed
250g/9oz white chocolate
3 egg whites

TOFFEE APPLE TART WITH ALMOND CRUMBLE

Toffee has a pull, be it toffee-coated popcorn, sticky toffee pudding, or the fudgy sweets wrapped in gold foil your grandma gave you – it's tempting because it's nostalgic.

SERVES 8

For the pastry

175g/6oz plain flour, plus
    extra to dust
1 generous pinch of salt
50g/2oz ground almonds
3 tbsp icing sugar
zest of 1 lemon
100g/3½oz cold unsalted
    butter
2 eggs yolks
1 tbsp full-fat milk

For the almond crumble

75g/3oz unsalted butter
100g/3½oz plain flour
½ tsp ground cinnamon
65g/2½oz brown sugar
50g/2oz ground almonds
30g/generous 1oz toasted
    flaked almonds

For the filling

1 tin of Carnation Caramel
2 large cooking apples,
    peeled, cored and finely
    sliced into segments

Treat your guests to a childhood revival with this fairground-inspired flan. Only this time, no one should lose a wobbly tooth in the caramel.

To make the pastry, mix the flour, salt, almonds, icing sugar, lemon zest and butter until crumbly – you can do this by hand or in a food processor. Add the egg yolks and milk and bring it together. Roll it into a ball and refrigerate for 1 hour – this helps keep the pastry nice and short and crumbly.

Once the chilling time is through, roll out the pastry on a lightly floured surface and use to line a 25.5cm/10in flan tin. Trim the edges and then refrigerate again for a further hour.

Preheat the oven to 180°C/350°F/gas 4. Take the pastry case out of the fridge and bake it blind for 15 minutes.

While it is baking, get on with the crumble mix, which really couldn't be simpler. Cream the butter, then add the flour and cinnamon until you have a crumb-like mixture. Add the sugar and almonds, ground and toasted, and mix well. Don't bother smoothing out any lumps – those add to the texture of the crumble.

Once the pastry base has baked, take it out of the oven and smear the caramel all over the bottom of it. Arrange the apples over the mixture and then bake again for 20 minutes. The apples should start to cook and the toffee should be bubbling. Finally, take the tart out of the oven and top with the crumble mix. Take the oven temperature up one notch, put the tart back into the oven and bake for a further 20 minutes.

Serve generous slices with a scoop of ice cream.

Acknowledgements

There are many people I have to thank for this book. First and foremost I would like to give credit to my wonderful family – Mum, your patience, love and wisdom are a gift unique to you. Thank you, Daddy, for always having an appetite for trying the new – your adventurous taste widened the horizons of my foodie world from an early age. I am indebted to my big sisters Jazz Rehal, Rashpal Nyotta and Charon Chawla – I am but an extension of all of you, and this book is a reflection of what you have taught me – your support and care has been unconditional. To my wonderful brother Harpreet – for tasting the good, the bad and the ugly on my daily menu with gusto – I love you for it. Also, to my grandmother – your tales and fables have fed my soul and imagination. I am grateful as well to my large extended family – brothers-in-law, nieces, nephews, aunts, uncles and cousins – I adore you all.

To my darling friend Heather Whyley – you continue to be a source of inspiration and magic – I love you. Also to the supers Shazia Ejaz and Sarita Bhatia – kisses of appreciation for championing me from the very beginning.

From the bottom of my heart I'd like to thank Felicity Blunt who lovingly nurtured this book – it blossomed under your careful tending and liberal vodka watering. Thank you for believing in me from sapling stage and always going above and beyond the call of duty. This would not be possible without you. Deep thanks also to Jacqui Drewe and all at Curtis Brown – for giving me a break when I needed one.

Heartfelt gratitude to everyone who worked so hard on this book including beautiful Carole Tonkinson – I have been blessed to have you – you are made from the stuff of author's fantasies. To Katy Carrington – your enthusiasm, energy and workhorse attitude even when you had morning sickness have been exemplary. Jacqui Caulton – superwoman – thanks for casting aside your housework to spend many extra hours on my book and doing such a fantastic job!

Jason Lowe – genius. You crafted in your extraordinary photographs what I couldn't put into words. Also fabulous Cynthia Inions – you brought your very own fragile magic to every day – thanks for lighting up everyone with your infectious personality and wit. Glorious Lori de Mori – I thank you for your love and wisdom – I couldn't have managed without you. Also lovely Celine for keeping us all sane in the kitchen.

To the brilliant Gordon Ramsay and Pat Llewellyn – I am full of gratitude to you both for the fine start you gave me. Thank you for believing in me.

A very big thank you also to Jill Wanless and Ali Hall for giving me so many opportunities and teaching me all about my reader. Your influence has been immense.

I owe thanks to a number of superb people for providing cooking equipment, notably Kitchen Aid, Kenwood and Argos – your generosity has enabled my recipes to take shape! Also to the creative shoe geniuses, *ensembliers* and fashionistas whose talent graces these pages – Christian Louboutin, Rupert Sanderson, Olivia Morris, Terry de Havilland, Strutt Couture, www.feathersfashion.com and www.start-london.com – I'd be skin and bones without you. Lucy Wood – you're a bright spark – thank you for supplying me with many a fashion moment. Thanks to gorgeous Lucy Martin at URPR for many a happy moment spent at the Urban Retreat.

Finally I'd like to humbly thank that one other whose presence in my life has been a constant in troubled times and in the good. Your blessings have been countless. I belong to you.

Index

illustrations are shown in **bold**